Here is a serious, scriptural answer to a thorny problem that is tearing the body of Christ to shreds. Rod Cooper writes not as a theorist but as one who has struggled personally with the incisive issues he surfaces. Don't expect a quick and easy sound-bite TV solution. Rather, the author offers a menu that is hard to swallow, harder still to implement, but impossible to ignore. Racial reconciliation is never an option to the Christian, but always an essential—and long overdue.

> Howard G. Hendricks
> Author, *As Iron Sharpens Iron*
> Chairman, Center for Christian Leadership

I first heard of Rod Cooper from my son Greg who, as his student, raved about this man's wisdom and loving character. Rod Cooper has done what should have been done years ago. He has taken the elements that make up a healthy family relationship and applied them to our nation. He not only explains why we have so much racial tension in our country today, but he shows us specifically what men can do to move closer to healing. He challenges us to take action within our own sphere of influence and move toward healthy relationships among men of all races.

> Gary Smalley
> Author, *The Hidden Value of a Man*

This book is for Christian men who feel incomplete and want to feel whole again. Rod Cooper suggests that the cure may not lie in looking inside ourselves. Rather, the remedy for wholeness lies in looking out at other members of Christ's body who we may not see at all. For Christ's sake, as well as your own, read this book and reap a new adventure-filled life.

> Haddon Robinson
> Howard John Ockenga Professor of Preaching
> Gordon-Conwell Theological Seminary

WE STAND TOGETHER

Reconciling Men

of Different

Color

RODNEY L. COOPER Ph.D.

MOODY PRESS

CHICAGO

To the one who has continually taught me
that "Jesus never fails,"
my mother, Avanell E. Cooper

ISBN: 0-8024-9181-2

Contents

Foreword

A war is underway in America, though few men will acknowledge it. African-American, Asian-American, American-Indian, Hispanic-American, and Anglo-American men all are at war with one another. The war is intense and highly destructive, yet most Christian men continue to play a role in it, usually unintentionally. The war builds dividing walls of hostility, and it's based on racism that creates a heavy atmosphere of hopelessness.

In this atmosphere, more and more Christian men are seeking for men of color and white men to live together as one in the church of Christ. There is hope for reconciliation, once we have understanding. *We Stand Together*, by Rodney Cooper, is a road map for this understanding.

I encourage men (and women) of all races and creeds to read this book. *We Stand Together* describes the war, identifies the warring parties, unwraps the causes, and diffuses the excuses. It also establishes a platform for understanding and shows the way for men to stand on godly common ground.

Reading this book, I have learned things about myself that have increased my ability to relate to other men—not just to men who are racially different, but also to men who are black like me. Rod's book is enhanced by the chapters contributed by Len, Jeff, Jesse, and Glenn, who provide handles for understanding as well as recommended solutions from their separate ethnic perspectives.

As Christian men we have ignored the signals that would help us to understand the plight of men in our country. There is no doubt that our peace and unity come through Christ and the finished work at Calvary. However, putting the biblical principle of reconciliation into practice is enhanced by understanding our social dynamics as men. My partner Glen Kehrein has said, "We didn't get into this mess by accident, and we're not going to get out of it by accident." Reconciliation requires positive, planned, and purposeful hard work.

Bill McCartney, founder of Promise Keepers, responded to a request by PK board members to speak on reconciliation by emphasizing a single phrase: "It's a war." Bill is right, and no general has ever won a war without having an astute analysis of the strengths, weaknesses, capabilities, and limitations of the enemy forces as well as his own. In this war of human relations, Rodney Cooper has removed the mask from the faces of all men.

As you read this book, you will come to understand men in their relationships to each other, and you will learn to exercise God's command to us all: to live out the ministry of reconciliation to men everywhere (2 Corinthians 5:18).

RALEIGH WASHINGTON
Coauthor of *Breaking Down Walls*

Foreword

God is clear about how He would have His children treat each other. In Leviticus we are told, "Do not hate your brother in your heart. . . . Do not seek revenge or bear a grudge against one of your people, but love your neighbor as yourself" (19:17–18). And Christ Himself declared to His followers: "A new command I give you: Love one another. As I have loved you, so you must love one another. By this all men will know that you are my disciples, if you love one another" (John 13:34–35).

Unfortunately, the long history of racism in America testifies to either an ignorance of or a refusal to acknowledge and obey God's unmistakably clear commandments. If God meant what He said, then it is clear that racism is sin! Yet racial division and strife continue as major problems in the 1990s—even among those who name Jesus Christ as Lord.

The good news is that God's Spirit is moving across our land, touching the hearts of Christians in a fresh way. He is calling us to humble ourselves, repent, and begin the process of healing and reconciliation. Many of God's people are beginning to move out of their comfort zones and to embrace racial reconciliation as a way to turn our world upside down for Christ.

But for a complete reconciliation to occur, there needs to be understanding. Not just between blacks and whites but with all men of color. Racism involves bias and prejudice from one ethnic group to another. *All* of us have bias and prejudice, driven by our fears and misunderstandings.

Rod Cooper breaks new ground with *We Stand Together*. He goes beyond information and exhortation to offer practical application. Cooper suggests that, if we look at America as a dysfunctional family, men of every minority group and even of the majority (white men) play different roles. From the white man as the enabler to the Hispanic man as the mascot, we all are acting out dysfunctional roles. We need each other to become whole again.

The dysfunctional roles are not necessarily those we chose. Yet because of stereotyping many Anglos and minorities end up, often unwillingly, playing these roles. Cooper and other contributors show how these roles deprive us of healthy relationships and hinder reconciliation. They show how we can open the system to become men who relate as God intended rather than through false stereotypes.

The mandate "To act justly and to love mercy and to walk humbly with your God" (Micah 6:8) should be our motto. This book emphasizes what men from each group must do personally to have solid relationships with those outside their own ethnic group.

This isn't a book by a black man for white men. It's a gift from Christian men of every race to each other to help us break out of the stereotypes that have bound us. It is written to help us to understand each other, love and support each other, and to begin to work together to become who God would have us to be.

"And do this, understanding the present time. The hour has come for you to wake up from your slumber, because our salvation is nearer now than when we first believed. The night is nearly over; the day is almost here. So let us put aside the deeds of darkness and put on the armor of light" (Romans 13:11–12). The salvation of our nation awaits the repentance and reconciliation of his people. Men can and must lead the way. Rod Cooper shows us how.

GARY J. OLIVER
Author of *Real Men Have Feelings Too*

Acknowledgments

This project would not have been possible were it not for a good brother who convinced me I had something worthwhile to say. That brother is Gary Oliver, Ph.D., director of Southwest Counseling Center and a gifted author. Gary is the general editor of the Men of Integrity series, also by Moody Press, which includes two books that I highly recommend on men's identity and developing friendships, *Real Men Have Feelings Too* and *Bonds of Iron*. Thanks, Gary, for your encouragement in this work.

I want to thank the four contributors to this book: Jeff King, Leonard Tamura, Jesse Miranda, and my soul brother, Glenn Wagner. It is their work that makes this book truly unique and valuable. I also want to thank Moody Press editor Jim Vincent for his wonderful suggestions and for making this book readable. Also, thanks to Cheryl Smith for the wonderful discussion questions.

Finally, thanks to Nancy, my wife, who kept encouraging me when the going got tough.

About the Contributors

The four contributors who have written chapters 4 through 7 of this book bring an insider's perspective to those chapters. Because each man is a member of the racial group he writes about, his discussion includes a personal understanding and empathy. And as a teacher and leader, each offers a scholar's knowledge and insights to his writings. Let me introduce you to them.

Jeff King, a tribally enrolled member of the Creek Nation of Oklahoma, is a licensed clinical psychologist. He lives in Denver, where he serves as codirector of Native American Counseling, providing counseling to the surrounding Native-American communities. King earned a Ph.D. degree in clinical psychology at Pennsylvania State University and teaches courses periodically at the University of Colorado, University of Denver, and Denver Seminary. He is also a staff psychologist at the University of Denver, providing multicultural training and counseling services to faculty, staff, and students.

Leonard Tamura, also a licensed clinical psychologist, is clinical director of pastoral counseling for Denver and the psychology training coordinator at the Asian/Pacific Center for Human Development in Denver. He counsels families and individual children and adults in a private practice, is associate professor at Colorado Christian University, and teaches occasionally at the University of Denver. He has a Ph.D. in clinical psychology and an M.A. in psychology from the Rosemead School of Psychology, La Mirada, California.

Jesse Miranda, a Hispanic leader living in southern California, teaches courses on leadership and urban ministry at Azusa Pacific University. He is associate dean of urban/multi-cultural affairs at the university, directing all ethnic programs and reaching into minority communities where he recruits students. Miranda is a member of the board of directors of Promise Keepers and serves as president of both *Alianza de Ministerios Evangelicos Nacionales* (AMEN) and the Hispanic Association for Theological Education. He has a D.Min. from Fuller Theological Seminary and has earned masters degrees in education (California State University) and religious education (Talbot Theological Seminary).

E. Glenn Wagner has helped to train leaders through several key positions, most recently as vice president in charge of national and international expansion of Promise Keepers. Wagner speaks at Men's Ministry Leadership Seminars and Promise Keepers conferences and is a contributor to the best-selling book *Seven Promises of a Promise Keeper*. He has served as an adjunct college and seminary professor and has a Ph.D. in religion and society from Oxford Graduate School, Dayton, Tennessee, an M.A. in counseling from Grace Graduate School, Long Beach, California, and has studied at Biblical Theological Seminary in Hatfield, Pennsyvania.

INTRODUCTION
Men Wanted
for Hazardous Journey

B ritish Antarctic explorer Sir Ernest Shackleton (1874–1922)
placed this advertisement in London newspapers in 1900 in
preparation for the National Antarctic Expedition (which subse-
quently failed to reach the South Pole):

> MEN WANTED FOR HAZARDOUS JOURNEY. Small wages, bitter cold,
> long months of complete darkness, constant danger, safe return doubt-
> ful. Honor and recognition in case of success—Ernest Shackleton.

Shackleton later said of the call for volunteers that "it seemed as
though all of the men in Great Britain were determined to accompany
me, the response was so overwhelming." The response to Ernest
Shackleton's advertisement shows clearly that men love adventure
and challenge. It shows that men love to take on what seems like insurmountable obstacles to say that they have "been there, done that,"
just for the thrill of it.

I am looking for the same kind of risk-takers Ernest Shackleton
was seeking for his expedition. Only the journey I am asking you to
take is even more hazardous—but also more rewarding. In fact, I can
guarantee that you will discover and experience incredible riches if
you decide to take the challenge. What is the challenge?

- To become men who are ministers of reconciliation.
- To overcome disunity caused by racism, stereotypes, and prejudice.
- To love one another as Christ has loved us.

To put the matter bluntly, the call is to act as members of the body of Christ should act.

The bottom line is that you are incomplete without knowing and accepting other men—Asian, black, Indian, Hispanic, and white—and they are incomplete without knowing you. We need each other to be whole in our manly identity. To put it another way, you cannot be all that God has called you to be without me, nor can I without you. First Corinthians 12 points out that we are one body. If one member of the body hurts, we all hurt. It is my responsibility to minister to you—no matter what the color—because you are part of my body.

THE SHARED MALE EXPERIENCE

It sounds simple, but it is not easy. Whoever said that being obedient to Christ's command to love one another would be easy? The journey I am asking you to take is extremely hazardous because we must look not only on the inside concerning our attitudes toward those who are different, but we must also fight the battle of establishing what it means to be a man in our society. We, as men, are living in a time when we are fighting for our lives as a gender. Sam Keen, in his book *Fire in the Belly,* put it well:

> Ask most any man "How does it feel to be a man these days? Do you feel manhood is honored, respected and celebrated?" Those who pause long enough to consider their gut feelings will likely tell you they feel blamed, demeaned and attacked. But their reactions may be pretty vague. Many men feel as if they are involved in a night battle in a jungle against an unseen foe. Voices from the surrounding darkness shout hostile challenges: "Men are too aggressive. Too soft. Too insensitive. Too macho. Too power-mad. Too much like little boys. Too wimpy. Too violent. Too obsessed with sex. Too detached to care. Too busy. Too rational. Too lost to lead. Too dead to feel." Exactly what are we supposed to become is not clear.[1]

Despite rumors to the contrary, men as a gender are being devastated physically, psychologically, emotionally, and spiritually by our society.

The examination of male roles has become established, even fashionable. There is now so much being written and said about men that the problem is no longer finding relevant material but determining what is important and true. Although there are many reasons that men are feeling confused, one seems to stand out: stereotypes. For instance, many times white men in our culture are pictured in the media as bumbling idiots, incompetent husbands, and inadequate fathers who are always being rescued by their more competent wives. Gary Oliver concludes that "White men have become the 'dumb blondes' of the nineties." It is these stereotypes that keep many white men hamstrung in regard to their identity and relationships.

Just as white men must battle the stereotypes placed upon them by society, men of color have been battling the stereotypes about them for decades. I should know. I am an African-American man who even in the evangelical Christian world has had to battle the stereotypes my white Christian brothers and sisters have put on me. Men who are African-American, Native-American, Asian-American, and Latino (or Hispanic) testify to the same struggles for acceptance, even within the body of Christ. You will be hearing from Jeff King (Native American), Leonard Tamura (Asian-American), Jesse Miranda (Hispanic), and Glenn Wagner (Anglo), along with me, Rod Cooper (African-American), concerning the key issues of acceptance, identity, and reconciliation. This book is unique because a man from each group shares his experiences with stereotypes and the disastrous effects they bring to the body of Christ.

The purpose of this book is primarily to challenge men of all races to tell Satan to "get thee behind me" when it comes to the stereotypes that keep us from being one in Christ. For this to happen, we must understand that all people have been created in the image of God. We all stand on an even playing field as far as God is concerned. I have no more—or less—of the image of God than my Hispanic, Asian, Indian, or white brothers. Rather than be separated by our ethnicity, we need to celebrate it. Yet men of different nations and colors love differently, have different goals and needs, and, like Anglos, are confused as to what it means to be a man.

Describing the United States as a melting pot—an overused expression—is suggestive of a country where people of every class, creed, and color with different customs have melded together to create a new culture. However, the United States is not now, and never was, some kind of homogenized culture where people from around the globe with their many differences somehow softened into a new kind of supraculture. Since its beginning, one and only one racial-ethnic group has dominated and become the standard for others to emulate—namely, Western Europeans.

George Barna, an expert in the study of social trends, points out in his book *The Frog in the Kettle* that by the year 2000 one in every three people in America will be a minority.[2] In the Los Angeles school district alone it has been found that more than eighty languages are spoken. For decades we have had more Jews than does the nation of Israel. There are more blacks in America than in any other nation in the world except Nigeria. Only Mexico and Spain have more Hispanic people than the United States. We truly live in a diverse and pluralistic world. Yet, if we do not value the cultural differences of other men, then we will likely take a defensive posture and see those differences as threatening rather than enriching.

We need to understand that being a member of a minority-racial group affects men's lives. Such analysis should lead us to yet another consideration; namely, there is no one masculine template for all males to follow. Rather, we must consider a man's race and how that affects his self-image and view of life.

We also need to understand that much of the devaluation and discomfort Anglo men feel today is very similar to what minority men have faced all their lives. Thus, more than ever reconciliation is possible between men of all races because of the tremendous sense of devaluation men as a gender are feeling.

WE ARE ONE IN THE SPIRIT, WE ARE ONE IN THE LORD

Each man's struggles, regardless of race, is significant and must not be minimized. Yet, the key to dealing with the struggles men are facing in society is to recognize that we are intricately tied to one another because of our heritage in Christ. Each man must value himself for who he is in Christ—namely, that our value as men is not in what we do or in who we know, but in whose we are. We are sons of God—children of the King. As Max Lucado wrote:

> Jesus' love does not depend upon what we do for Him. Not at all. In the eyes of the King you have value simply because you are. You don't have to look nice or perform well. Your value is inborn. Period. Think about that for just a minute. You are valuable simply because you exist. Not because of what you do or what you have done, but simply because you are. Remember that the next time you are left bobbing in the wake of someone's steamboat ambition. Remember that the next time some trickster tries to hang a bargain basement price tag on your self-worth. The next time someone tries to pass you off as a cheap buy, just think about the way Jesus honors you . . . and smile.[3]

Reconciliation is not an option or a suggestion—it is a command. First Corinthians 5:18 declares that God has given us the ministry of reconciliation. It is God's desire to have a healthy church that demonstrates love, respect, and honor toward each one of its members. The apostle Paul exhorted the Ephesian believers:

> I urge you to live a life worthy of the calling you have received. Be completely humble and gentle; be patient, bearing with one another in love. Make every effort to keep the unity of the Spirit through the bond of peace. There is one body and one spirit—just as you were called to one hope when you were called—one Lord, one faith, one baptism; one God and father of all. (4:1–6)

Jesus gave all of Himself to reconcile us to Himself and to teach others. He valued us that much. Can we afford to do any less? If we value ourselves as God does, then we in turn can value others because we see them as the Lord sees them. If we do not value ourselves ("Love your neighbor as yourself," Leviticus 19:18), then we end up competing over whose struggle is the most difficult and, as a result, resort to stereotyping each other to justify our position as being the most important.

> After this I looked and there before me was a great multitude that no one could count, from every nation, tribe, people and language, standing before the throne and in front of the Lamb. They were wearing white robes and were holding palm branches in their hands. And they cried out in a loud voice:
>
> > "Salvation belongs to our God,
> > who sits on the throne,
> > and to the Lamb."
>
> The apostle John, Revelation 7:9–10 NIV

We all will be one in heaven. Yet God has called us to be a reflection of heaven right now on earth. Join me in the journey. You will receive honor and recognition from the one who matters most—Jesus. We can do it because "greater is He who is in [us] than he who is in the world" (1 John 4:4).

CHAPTER ONE
All in the Family

J im, a successful businessman, was an African-American who en- joyed all the trappings of his success. He had the nice office, coun- try club membership, and dressed in the latest fashions. Yet he had come to me for counseling as an angry man. His wife had moved out with the kids and was having an affair. Even though he had made it to the top in his profession in terms of position, money, and status, he now found himself alone and out of control.

What had happened? As we talked, it became clear his anger stemmed from his false sense of manhood. He had swallowed the caricature of cultural masculinity, the one that paints the "real man" as being: (1) autonomous, (2) efficient, (3) intensely goal-oriented, (4) emotionally detached, and (5) separated from the community. Jim, at the top of his business career, had swallowed the lie and found him- self emotionally bankrupt and alone.

Many men in our society feel as Jim did: alienated, powerless, and angry. Perhaps you feel that way too. All men deal with the de- mons of insecurity, selfishness, and despair no matter their race or heritage. Still, we cannot ignore our backgrounds. Your socioecono- mic status and race influences who you are and what you fear. Equally important, the background of other men influences you greatly.

This book is not about how men of different races deal with their struggles, although that will be touched upon. It is about understand- ing your own struggles and how those struggles affect your own identity and how you perceive men whose backgrounds are different than your own. It is also about understanding other men's struggles with their masculinity and how their struggles affect their identity and their perception of you.

Why is this important? Because in reading about other men's and our own masculinity we men can help each other know ourselves better, serve God and each other in love—as we are called to do—and to accept one another in the process.

OUR RELATIONSHIPS AND OUR VALUES

Sadly, American society has limited the ways white men and men of color can deal with their specific issues. The way we deal with relationships has a lot to do with Anglo-Saxon values, expectations, and standards. Not all are correct; typically they are simply Anglo-Saxon in nature. Those men of other minority groups are expected to conform, but even those in the majority group can find their expectations not always reasonable.

Let me give you an example. Larry was thirty-five, the father of two children, and had been married for ten years. He was very active in his church; in fact, he directed the men's ministry in his church. He had just given a birthday party for his daughter, who had turned age five, when he began having panic attacks. Larry could sleep little and often felt anxious.

He memorized Scripture, prayed, and told his wife about his concerns, which certainly helped, but he continued to have the panic attacks. Finally his wife suggested he go see a Christian counselor. With great reluctance he came to see me, and I began to ask him a few questions.

"How long have you experienced these panic attacks?"

"For about three weeks, beginning right after my daughter's birthday party."

"If you don't mind, I'd like to get from you your family history. Sometimes we bury events that have been painful in our past. Sometimes a similar event later will stir up the event we have been stuffing, and we begin to experience all those painful feelings."

We talked, and Larry emphasized to me that he had not been sexually or physically abused. He was adamant that his family loved him and that he came from a fine Christian home. He thought nothing in his past was making him feel anxious.

"OK, but can we at least give it a try?"

Larry protested but finally consented to try. I asked him to relax and think about early events that may have influenced him. All of a sudden he sat up and began to get teary eyed.

"I know why I am panicky. When I was five years old my mother gave me a birthday party. For some reason I did something that displeased my mother. So she sat me down and drew on a piece of paper a large circle. She then drew lines through the circle to where it looked like slices of a pie. She then said, 'Every time I color in one of these slices it means you have been bad. And if/when I color all of them in it means God doesn't love you anymore. So you better be good.'"

Larry realized he had panicked because he did not want his daughter to experience the same fear of rejection that he felt on that day. He did not want to be the cause of his daughter's pain.

Larry also realized that he had accepted several erroneous rules during his conversation with his mother on his fifth birthday. He learned, incorrectly of course, that God expected him to perform and not make mistakes or He would leave him. He also learned to play the role of the "perfect child." Our family often determines the rules we have about life, the roles we play in life, and the quality of our relationships throughout life.

One truth Larry learned was how an individual can impact the feelings of others. His mother had created fear and sadness for her little boy. His family sent him certain messages that influenced the way he went about relating to others and resolving (or not resolving) his issues. Through understanding how his family impacted him he could find healing.

You too have values that come from the family with whom you have kinship. Most men, whether of Asian, black, Hispanic, or white background, struggle for purpose as husbands or unmarried adults as they sort through their values. What values do you have? Are they correct?

If we are Christians who seek to honor Jesus Christ, we will recognize that all values, including those of the majority Anglo culture, at times conflict with heavenly values. Your background, like Larry's, shapes your values and responses to events, but those responses rarely are superior to the responses of others. We must learn to respect and honor the group values of our brothers, which often differ from our own. To see the limitations of our own values and the worth of other perspectives, we need a basic understanding of how a family shapes its members' roles and perspectives. When we do that, we will better understand our place as men and honor the perspectives of Christians of other backgrounds.

Most Christians are strongly influenced by their families of origin. In this chapter we will consider how family dynamics affect the roles we play as adults.

IT'S A FAMILY MATTER

The family is like a factory, writes sociologist Virginia Satir. In this factory, parents and environment help to produce either a healthy or unhealthy person. Four aspects of family life that strongly influence a person's development, according to Satir, are:

1. the feelings and ideas one has about oneself, which I call self-worth;
2. the ways people work out to make meaning with one another, which would be called communication;
3. the rules people use for how they should feel and act, which eventually develops into what is called their role in life;
4. the way people relate to other people and institutions outside the family, which would be called their world view or link to society.

Interestingly, in the troubled families she observed, Satir consistently saw the following characteristics:

1. self-worth was low;
2. communication was indirect, vague, and not really honest;
3. rules were rigid, inhuman, non-negotiable, and everlasting;
4. their world view concerning society was fearful, placating, and blaming.[1]

These characteristics, in essence, are the characteristics of a dysfunctional family. As we study the five main racial groups in the United States—African-, Asian-, Hispanic-, Native- and the dominant Euro-American, we will discover that the above four characteristics display themselves in differing degrees in all five groups. The way these characteristics are displayed has a lot to do with the role each one has seemingly been assigned to play in society. Most significantly, for us to be healthy and whole men, we need to interact with and accept each other, letting someone else's strength balance our weakness. Together, we can become a healthier family. We men need each other.

When we are willing to develop friendships with men of other backgrounds, we move toward becoming a healthy family, a family in which nurturing predominates. What does a healthy family look like?

The relationships in the family are more important than the roles. Satir describes a vibrant, healthy family with all four traits in the positive column:

1. self-worth is high;
2. communication is direct, clear, specific, and honest;
3. rules are flexible, human, appropriate and subject to change;
4. their world view concerning society is open, hopeful and optimistic.[2]

These characteristics are largely lacking in men as a whole and in minority men in particular. You see, America seems to have more of an environment of a dysfunctional family than a healthy family. Satir's criteria for a healthy versus an unhealthy family has been expanded to what is now called a "closed" family system versus an "open" family system.

THE CLOSED FAMILY SYSTEM

The closed system has ten key areas that describe the way a closed family operates compared to an open family system. As I indicated, most men operate in an unhealthy family system, or a closed system. Let's look at several categories and ways the closed system seems to impact relationships, especially racial relationships.

A Closed Family

Four major elements of the closed-style family are (1) a closed family, (2) tense and negative emotional atmosphere, (3) rigid thoughts, beliefs, and values, and (4) resistance to change and growth. The first element, the basic family system, requires conformity and obedience to rigid rules, values, and expectations. In fact, the closed system punishes "wrongdoing" and is mostly concerned about status, appearance, roles, and reputation.

I have a friend, Jeff, who is black and happily married to Janet, who is white. Jeff often stores a shotgun in the trunk of his car for protection. He told me a couple of times he has been run off the road because he was not supposed to be with a white woman. He was not conforming to the rules. A few people implied that his being with a white woman did not look right. Jeff's experiences and his response—to protect his wife and himself—show how strong those rules and expectations can be.

A Negative Emotional Atmosphere

The second element in the closed-style family is a negative emotional amosphere. The emotional atmosphere is tense and defensive;

family members are typically insensitive to the feelings of others as well as being critical, blaming others for problems in their lives. Members tend to be judgmental, guilt-producing, and boring.

In race relations, this leads to misunderstanding, tension, and in its worst form, violence. On June 19, 1982, Vincent Chin, a Chinese-American, was beaten to death with a baseball bat by two white male auto workers. According to witnesses, the two men mistook Chin as being Japanese and blamed him for the loss of jobs in the U.S. auto industry. Prior to the fatal beating, the men were heard to make angry racial slurs at Chin. The two men were convicted of manslaughter but were sentenced to only three years of probation and a fine of $3,750.00 each. The incident and sentence drew a storm of protest from the Asian community and prompted some to say "An Asian's life is worth only $3,750.00 in this country."[3]

Also, as recent as 1992 there have been racial incidents on college campuses and universities, supposed bastions of enlightenment. In one incident a cross was burnt in a black student's dormitory room, a reminder of the Ku Klux Klan's intimidation of African-Americans; in another football players at Dartmouth College taunted a black female as she walked by their practice facility, calling her "dark meat."[4] Truly the emotional atmosphere between the races is tight and defensive, perhaps even worse than it has ever been.

Rigid Thoughts, Beliefs, and Values

A third element of the closed system concerns thoughts, beliefs, and values. Certain ideas and values are rigidly held and defended, and contrary or different views are often unacceptable. The range of interests is narrow.

This happens usually when the minority person's viewpoint comes into conflict with the majority Anglo-Saxon viewpoint. For instance, I was having a conversation with some of my white teaching colleagues at seminary a couple years ago. The topic was the qualifications of a minority person, a Chinese, who was a candidate for an academic position at our school. One of my colleagues, who sat on the committee to interview the candidate, said, "I asked him what he felt were the three most pressing social issues of our day. He rated racism as number one, socioeconomic issues as number two, and women's issues as number three."

According to my colleague, another committee member expressed surprise that the candidate did not mention abortion among his top three. "Isn't abortion really the key issue we should be battling?" the member asked.

It seemed to my white colleague that the only real social issue worth pursuing was the abortion issue. I also remember being in a conversation with some of my white friends where I mentioned that the abortion issue was not the only issue. I said, "What about those who are disadvantaged and racism?"

"Come on, Rod, get real," one of my friends answered. "Those other issues are good issues to pursue, but abortion is truly a biblical issue." I was in essence being told I was not being biblical in pursuing other social issues and therefore unacceptable.

Resistance toward Change and Growth

A fourth aspect of the closed style of family is resistance toward change. In this area individuals cling to the status quo. In race relations, this shows itself when people in positions of power and authority resist changes in the workplace when minorities want greater participation. For instance, many minority men feel that as soon as they start to excel on the job they bump into a "glass ceiling." In a 1984 *Time* magazine cover story entitled "Between Two Worlds," one photo caption read "The Black middle-class has everything the white middle-class has, except a feeling it really fits in."

This is not unique to blacks. Film actor Bruce Lee, an Asian American, became very successful in the television series "The Green Hornet" as the sidekick to this comic book character. Later, Lee introduced an idea for a Chinese Kung Fu specialist to wander the wild West and be the main character of the show. The name of the series was to be called "Kung Fu." As recalled in his movie biography *Dragon: The Bruce Lee Story,* a white man was cast for the part instead of Bruce Lee. Bruce Lee was reminded that he was to stay in "his place." His idea was OK, but he was not the actor to play the role, even though Lee was trained in the martial arts, had performed in a series of Kung Fu movies, and came up with the idea. His taking a leading role in a TV series represented too much of a change.

Other Traits of a Closed Family System

The closed style of family living can be seen in six other categories. Though they describe a nuclear family with parents and children, they also apply to adult men, our brothers created like us to have fellowship with each other and our God, no matter our race. Do any of these six elements describe you in your relationship with your family? Do they describe your relationship with other men?

1. *Family behavior patterns.* The family interactions become (pro-grammed) repetitive, restrictive, and limiting.

2. *Family communication patterns.* The way the family communi-cates is often limited, distorted, and ineffective. Family members have poor listening skills, and communication often is cut off by critical or judgmental remarks. The members of the family often are unable or unwilling to share "deeper" feelings.

3. *Family decision-making patterns.* One member overrides wishes or preferences of others, or there is unsatisfying compromise.

4. *Roles in the family.* Typically the roles are stereotyped, unequal, and resistant to change. There is the "man's role," "woman's role," and "child's role." Often unfair division of work and responsibility. We will see how this pertains to minority men in a later section.

5. *Parent-child relationships.* With small children, the parents dictate, discipline, and punish for wrongdoing. They view the child's role as to obey, be good, conform, have neat appearance, and respect his elders. The goal is to indoctrinate the child as to what to think and believe. The child is even taught how to feel and how to live. The child typically is treated as a possession and an object; his feel-ings ignored. There are frequent reprimands and punishments or else neglect. Love is often conditional on behavior.

   When the child becomes a teenager, the parents continue to be authoritative but can rarely make it work. Mutual insensitivity and poor communication are common, and the teen is filled with re-sentment.

6. *Attitudes toward people and society.* People, typically are viewed in terms of status, roles, sex, race, politics, etc., but not primarily as individual human beings. In fact, there are suspicions toward out-side relationships; those living in a closed family regard society as being separate and "out there."[5]

AN OPEN FAMILY SYSTEM

An Open style

The goal, of course, is an open system. Here the basic family system is democratic, flexible, nurturing, and freedom-granting. The family members are seen as persons, and their feelings and needs are recognized. The open-style family encourages each person to grow and be all that they can be.

I have a good friend who was offered a promotion. The promo-tion would mean greater prestige for him and more income for his family. Furthermore, if he did not take it he would possibly be passed over for future positions. He held a "Family Council," seeking the input of his wife and children about a potential move to a new state, a new home. At the time his children were in their junior and senior years in high school. His wife also had a solid network of good friends. Each family member expressed a desire to stay. After much prayer and thought he decided not to take the position. I asked him what was the deciding factor.

"Rod, God has called me to create an environment where my family can grow and flourish. Just as you would not take a healthy flower that is blooming from the fertile soil it occupies, so also it would be foolish for me to take my family out of the fertile soil that is producing such quality and character in my kids and wife. Besides, I can always get another job—but I cannot always have the environment I have for my family right now." My friend, who happens to be white, operated from an open style concerning his family.

The elements of an open family style all contribute to healthy family members. The *emotional atmosphere feels comfortable* and safe. There is a spontaneity in the family where feelings are expressed freely and fun can break out at any time. There is an atmosphere where people just enjoy one another. *Thoughts, beliefs, and values are flexible.* There are no "untouchable" areas that cannot be discussed. There is a willingness to listen to other views as well as respect for differences and uniqueness. Also, there is a flexibility to change positions where appropriate.

In an open style of family, *family communication patterns are clear,* open, and effective. There is a freedom to go "deep" with one another and share feelings. People feel listened to in this system and are not cut-off. *Decision making* takes everyone's needs into account. There is no sense of being left out. The *roles in the family are flexible.* For instance, I remember my father would do the dishes after dinner just so Mom could rest and relax. No one had an attitude that the dishes were "women's" work.

Furthermore, *parent-child relationships are positive.* Children are seen as persons in their own right. They are encouraged to question, think, feel, and dream. There is mutual trust and safety. *Attitudes toward people and society are positive.* People are seen as people. They are not seen stereotyped into broad categories such as "all black are. . . ." Finally, *change and new experiences are seen as opportunities.* The world is a place to be explored—not to fear.

THE CLOSED SYSTEM AND MINORITY MEN

Admittedly, the open and closed systems are on the extreme ends of a continuum. Some families may contain characteristics of both or be nearer to either end of the continuum in some areas than in others.

Yet, I believe that most men, especially minority men, feel that they are trapped—trapped in a closed system and relegated to fulfill certain roles, no matter how well they may progress up the ladder of socioeconomic success.

In fact, many minority men feel the very same feelings that an individual feels who comes from a dysfunctional family, no matter where they are on the socioeconomic ladder. They are: (1) a low self-worth; (2) a sense of powerlessness or the inability to change rules which are rigidly held concerning life and relationships; and (3) anger.

Such a closed system results in the three rules that are common to most dysfunctional families: (1) do not trust, (2) do not feel, and (3) do not talk. Those are also the very rules by which most minority men live their lives.

It is amazing how minority people, especially men, have learned to live by these rules. For example, if a group of African-Americans completed a personality test and the results indicated that as a group they were more suspicious than their white counterparts, how would the results be interpreted? Some psychologists and educators might use such information to label blacks as paranoid. They would argue that statements by blacks (such as those argued during the 1993 L.A. riots after the Rodney King verdict) that "'The Man' is out to get us" may be perceived as supporting a paranoid delusion. This interpretation, however, has been challenged by many black psychologists. Many blacks have experienced in their past and present history discrimination and subtle forms of prejudice by whites in positions of authority, these experts argue, so being suspicious or "paranoid" is not pathological but necessary for survival. "Playing it cool" has been identified as one means by which many black men conceal their true feelings and thoughts (remember the rules: do not trust—do not talk) so as not to feel vulnerable and be exploited.

Remember the category of a family system called "Attitudes toward change and society"? Such attitudes are sometimes called a person's worldview. For most minority men, the world is seen as a threatening place—a place where trust does not come easily.

PLAYING ROLES IN THE CLOSED SYSTEM

If most minority men feel that they are in a closed system—how do they survive in it? They must accept certain roles in order to find structure and predictability to their lives. Family systems theorists have come up with various roles in a dysfunctional or alcoholic family: (1) the enabler, (2) the hero, (3) the scapegoat, (4) the lost child, and (5) the mascot.

The Enabler

The enabler is the person in the family who provides responsibility and makes choices to compensate for the those who feel powerless and dependent. This person often does not see the illness or problems in the family, and when he does he feels guilty and tries to compensate by taking care of the person who is dependent or has the problem.

The Hero

The hero is the high achiever in the family, getting good grades, excelling in sports, and having a lot of interests outside of the family. Heroes are interested in looking good and presenting themselves as "together" to the outside world. They are dependable and well organized. They are skilled at people-pleasing and charming others. They are perfectionistic and come across as the ones who bring pride to the dysfunctional family.

The Scapegoat

The scapegoat will accept negative attention rather than no attention at all. He usually is perceived as the person who's always in trouble or likely to get into trouble. He appears to be irresponsible and defiant. He may be involved in the legal system at an early age, run away from home, be expelled from school for truancy, failing grades, or repeated offenses of bad behavior. If anyone is to be blamed for something, he gets the blame.

The Lost Child

The lost child will retreat to himself to cope with the frustrations of life. Usually quiet and withdrawn, he feels unimportant within the family structure. The quiet, lonely lost child can remain almost invisible and is treated as such.

The Mascot

The mascot assumes the role of comic relief and comforter within the family. He receives a lot of attention by being caring and fun-loving. This person presents a very nonresponsible exterior to the world, and his fun-loving nature usually keeps him from being taken seriously.

Each of these roles serves a purpose in the family, and sometimes one person may combine two of the roles. If we were to apply these roles on a broader scale within our society, who would play what roles? Interestingly, in American society each of these roles does have a place among men. As an African-American, Asian-American, Hispanic American, Native-American, or even Anglo-American, you either play or are assigned one of these roles.

Which one? Turn the pages to find out—and to find how you can break free of the stereotypical perceptions that come with the roles and start building healthy relationships with each other.

TAKE ACTION

1. Which of the ten elements of a closed family describes you?

2. Look at the five roles within the closed family. Which role, if any, have you played? How has it affected your ability to have solid relationships?

CHAPTER TWO

Warning: Being Black and Male Could Be Hazardous...

A young man in his late teens explained his predicament to the television reporter: "I was born a suspect. I came out of my mother's stomach, and anything that happened within a three-block radius, I was the suspect.

"White America is so scared of black teenagers. I walk down the streets, and women are like grabbing hold of their mace, and everybody's tucking in their chains. Everybody's getting into their car doors, and big 300-pound white guys start flexing, trying to scare me. First of all, I weigh 120 pounds soaking wet, holding a brick. I asked this guy for the time and he gave me his watch."[1]

SUSPICIONS AND PREJUDICE

The black teenager's comments, broadcast on public television's "MacNeil/Lehrer NewsHour," reflect not just an ugly stereotype but the prejudices that many whites have toward black males. The prejudice is not confined to teens. All African-American males, men and teenagers alike, encounter fear, alienation, and injustice in their daily dealings.

Darwin Davis, an older African-American who is a major executive with Equitable Life Assurance Society, explains the anger many supposedly successful blacks feel:

> There's an air of frustration [among young black managers] that's just as high now as it was 30 years ago.... They have even worse problems than I did because they've got M.B.A.s from Harvard. They did all

the things that you're supposed to do and things are supposed to happen.[2]

For instance, author Ellis Cose reported how one successful corporate lawyer encountered prejudice despite his qualifications:

> He had arrived at the office earlier than usual and entered the elevator along with a young white man. They got off at the same floor. No secretaries or receptionists were yet in place. As the black lawyer turned toward the locked outer office doors, his (white) elevator mate asked, "May I help you?" The black lawyer shook his head and attempted to circle around his would-be helper, but the young man stepped in front of him and demanded in a loud and decidedly colder tone, "May I help you?" At this time, the older (black) man fixed him with a stare, spat out his name, and identified himself as a partner, whereupon his inquisitor quickly stepped aside.

The black lawyer expressed anger that because of the younger man's color (white), "He felt he had the right to check me out." The black lawyer shook his head and said,

> "Here I am, a black man who has done all of the things I was supposed to do." He then proceeded to tick off what he had done: gone to Harvard, labored for years to make his mark in an elite law firm, married a highly motivated woman who herself had an advanced degree and a lucrative career. He and his wife were in the process of raising three exemplary children. Yet he was far from fulfilled.[3]

The lawyer's story was one of many in a 1993 *Newsweek* cover package entitled, "The Hidden Rage of Successful Blacks." The subjects, middle- to upper middle-class blacks, discussed how they had achieved great success but still were being perceived as second-class citizens.

The limits placed on African-Americans even exist in America's seemingly innocent pasttime, baseball. In an effort to acknowledge the historic breaking of the color barrier in baseball, Ted Koppel, host of ABC television's "Nightline," asked L.A. Dodgers executive Al Campanis why there were not more black executive managers and coaches in baseball. His answer was that blacks lack the "right stuff" to become front office executives. The interview, carried on national television, drew a howl of protests from minorities throughout the United States as evidence of racism in the power structures of baseball.

The author of this book, being African-American, has also experienced the sting of the "suspect" attitude that is often held toward black men. During college I learned that the best thing I could do was "overcome" or hide my blackness. I was the only black who lived on the floor of this all-male and all-white dormitory. I got into a conversation with a student about grades. He asked me how I was doing, and I told him I was pulling a 4.0 that quarter—straight A's. Without missing a beat he congratulated me. As we continued our conversation he tried to encourage me by saying that I was not like the rest of "them" (meaning blacks). I was an exception. His message was clear—being black is not something to rejoice about; it is something to overcome or hide.

A comment made by the black deputy mayor of New York City seems to sum up the feeling many black men are experiencing. "No matter what I accomplish as an individual, I will always be judged by what people see first, my color."[4]

"Who could, with a straight face, contend that black men are no longer the objects of scorn, suspicion, and political disenfranchisement?" asks Professor Bill Pannel in his book *The Coming Race Wars*. "Though the tactics have become more subtle, society still sends a clear message to black males that they are guilty before proven innocent."[5]

NOT GOOD ENOUGH

No matter how much a black man has achieved, he still feels that it is not quite good enough. Black men, before doing anything, usually must overcome tremendous stereotypes of inferiority and laziness that are based solely on their color.

In our model of the dysfunctional family, we are using the closed system to look at men of racial minorities. Within this system, the blacks typically play the role of the Scapegoat. According to Webster's New World Dictionary, a scapegoat is "a person or thing made to bear the blame for the mistakes or sins of others." If a man is seen in this light would it not affect one's self-image and overall worldview?

PERSISTENT IMAGES: THE BLACK DOLL STUDY

In 1939 psychologists Clark and Clark found some surprising results in their classic study called the "white doll/black doll" experiment.[6] The two researchers told black and white children, approximately five and six years of age, to choose to play with a white or black doll. Later they asked the children a series of questions, including "Which doll would you want to be like?" Black and white children both chose the white doll because, they said, the white doll was "prettier and smarter," whereas the black doll was "stupid and ugly." Both black and white children made these comments.

The experimenters would take the children, one by one, into a room and place both dolls in front of the child. Both the black and white children would quickly pick up the white doll and tell of its virtues—fine hair, nice skin, and overall a good person. When given the black doll, the children would quickly put the black doll down and say it was bad. In fact, the results of the study showed (1) black children preferred playing with the white dolls over the black one, (2) the black doll was perceived as being "bad," and (3) approximately one-third of the children, when asked to pick the doll that looked like them, picked the white one, even though they were black.

A lot of strides have taken place in regard to race relations since that experiment. One might expect that the results of such an experiment would be much different now following civil rights legislation and education concerning ethnic groups in this country. In fact, this same experiment was performed again in 1987, with Cabbage Patch dolls, and to everyone's surprise the results were better, in that many of the black children chose black dolls, but the attitude concerning being black had not changed significantly.[7]

As an Anglo-American, Asian-American, Hispanic-American, or Native-American, you may have the same attitudes toward black men. And even as an African-American, you and other blacks may wonder if you are ignorant, ugly, or the reason for certain problems in society. Why? Why are African-Americans, especially African-American men, seen as the scapegoat and feel so disenfranchised and unaccepted?

There are several reasons we often feel negative toward black men and they often feel negative toward themselves. Let me explain.

THE "BLACK SHEEP" OF THE FAMILY

As a family counselor, I have found that many of my clients still struggle with the way their original family perceives and treats them despite the amount of growth in their lives. For instance, if a boy was perceived or labeled as a troublemaker while growing up, that stigma often remains with him as an adult when encountering family members, no matter how much he has changed.

As a result, the person will either live up to (or down to) the label assigned to him, or he will spend the rest of his life trying to disprove the label. Yet, even if he disproves the label, it will often be seen as an exception rather than the rule.

That's what happened when my college dormmate complimented me for having straight A's one quarter. "Great. Good for you! I'm glad you're not like the rest of them. You're studying and it's paying off." When a black man is regarded as an exception to the rule, he then feels like he's in a no-win situation. *Most blacks still don't study,* his friend thinks, so even if a black student does well with his grades so far, he remains part of a group that generally does poorly in academics, according to others.

Sadly, this same attitude of "prove yourself different" affects all ethnic minorities. The historical and current experiences of racism and oppression in the United States make minority men feel culturally different and inferior. The past has a major impact on the present.

What has been the past history that has shaped the present of the black male? Here are highlights from Turner and Singleton's chart of racial beliefs during American history.

RACIAL BELIEFS DURING AMERICAN HISTORY

Period	Key Beliefs In Mainstream Culture
Slavery and Racial Oppression	
to 1650 (English heritage)	Blackness is evil in eyes of God.
1650–1760 (colonial America)	Black "animalistic" nature needs control.
1760–1820 (revolutionary era)	Slavery is necessary because blacks cannot manage their own freedom.
1820–1860 (pre–Civil War)	Slavery is good for the development of the nation and is a means to "protect" uncivilized and dependent blacks.
Racial Oppression	
1860–1914 (Civil War and Reconstruction)	The failure of blacks to achieve positive advancement in the mainstream culture confirms their basic inferiority. Their inability to use available opportunities necessitates supervision and control to prevent degeneration to a primitive state.
1914–1941 (World War I to World War II)	The inferiority of blacks is confirmed by scientific research, for example, in the areas of evolutionary theory and psychological testing. Continued racial segregation is necessary.

SOURCE: J. H. Turner and R. Singleton, Jr., "A Theory of Ethnic Oppression," *Social Forces* 56 (June 1978): 1001–8.

Turner and Singleton describe two additional periods of black history, the times of "Civil Rights Promises" (1948–1968) and "Moderation and Readjustment" (1968 to the present).[8] They argue that the progress during the Civil Rights Era was mitigated by a time of Moderation and Readjustment.

ALWAYS THE SCAPEGOAT

The accomplishments of the twenty years of the civil rights period were notable, yet we cannot expect a race of people to throw off in twenty years what three hundred years has produced in their psyche and their role in society. Indeed, that is the case: the black male still is seen as the scapegoat. And in a classic case of "blaming the victim," he is regarded as lacking "motivation" and therefore not getting ahead, according to Turner and Singleton.

This corresponds with the role in a dysfunctional family, where in trying to change his role from scapegoat, he causes others in the family to become uncomfortable. As a result, they put pressure on the member trying to change to get back in his "former role" so that they do not have to change.

Good and Bad, Black and White

The English language itself contributes to the black man being regarded as the scapegoat. Consider the words we use to describe good versus evil or right versus wrong. Our English dictionary connotes "white" as good and "black" as evil. In *Roget's Thesaurus of the English Language,* for example, the word *whiteness* has 134 synonyms, forty-four of which are favorable and pleasing to contemplate, including *purity, cleanness, bright, shining, ivory, stainless, clean, chaste, unblemished, unsullied, innocent, honorable,* and *straightforward.* Only ten synonyms for whiteness appear to have negative implications—and these only in the mildest sense: *gloss over, whitewash, gray, wan, pale,* etc.

The word *blackness* on the other hand has 120 synonyms, sixty of which are distinctly unfavorable, and none of them even mildly positive. Among them are such words as *blot, smudge, foreboding, forbidden, sinister, baneful, dismal, evil, wicked, malignant, deadly, unclean, dirty,* and *foul,* not to mention twenty synonyms directly related to race, such as *Negro, Negress, nigger,* and *darky.*

Ossie Davis, a playwright and actor, says concerning language:

When you consider the fact that thinking itself is sub-oral speech—in other words, one must use words in order to think at all—you will appreciate the enormous heritage or racial prejudgment that lies in wait for any child born into the English language. Any teacher good or bad, white or black, Jew or Gentile, who uses the English language as a medium of communication is forced willy-nilly to teach the Negro child 60 ways to despise himself and the white child 60 ways to aid and abet him in the crime."[9]

If one's self-image is shaped by social forces, by one's past history, then both black and white learn early to associate just the term "black" with inferiority or scapegoat terminology. The bad guys wear black clothes. When we went to church we heard that sin is black, when in reality the Bible addresses sin as "scarlet" and "crimson." Wordless books that used solid colors to teach us about sin and salvation informed us that our hearts were black. Only one phrase in our language implies that *black* is good—we have enough money to be out of debt when we are in the "black" financially.

Media Madness

Another reason for the scapegoat role is the depiction of blacks in the popular media, especially television. Both news shows and nightly TV series rarely show healthy black families led by healthy black men. Most of the models shown in the media concerning black men were pimps, hustlers, street corner men, drug dealers, and petty criminals.

I will never forget the famous Willie Horton commercial that helped elect George Bush the president in 1988. Republican strategists cited Horton as a casebook study of what was wrong with the criminal justice system. Horton had been sentenced to a lengthy term for murder but still qualified for the furlough program, which allowed him to leave prison for specified periods. During one furlough, he took off for Maryland, where he broke into a home of a white couple and then proceeded to tie up the man and brutally rape the woman.

All of this happened while Michael Dukakis, the 1988 Democratic presidential candidate, was the governor of Massachusetts. Dukakis was not directly aware of Horton's eligibility for furlough. Even so, those managing the Bush campaign made sure Horton was mentioned in advertisements and speeches.

There is no question that Horton's actions were reprehensible and should have been punished. But there was the racial aspect. Willie Horton was black; his Maryland victims were white. This was played upon in the Bush campaign and further stigmatized black men as being violent criminals. The campaign strategists who conceived and promoted the use of the TV ad may not have intended to use the Horton incident to smear black men or pander to the scapegoat mentality. If they did not see the ad as an attack, however, that proves how much they have accepted the white stereotyping of blacks, as they may have thought, *We're just reporting how some blacks treat whites.*

This scapegoat mentality is largely based on seeing crimes involving violence, particularly murder, robbery, and rapes, as "black crimes." But what about "white crime?" As Andre Hacker notes in *Two Nations: Black and White, Separate, Hostile and Unequal,* there is a bias in arresting and imprisoning blacks:

> Blacks comprise only about 12 percent of the population, [yet] they account for a high proportion—61.2 percent—of all robbery arrests. And they include over half of the suspects arrested for wrongful deaths, and close to half in cases of rape. Overall, black arrest rates are disproportionate for every offense except drunken driving.[10]

The high arrest rates have affected the levels of imprisonment. Whereas inmate populations in 1930 were 76.7 percent white and 22.4 percent black, over the years the level for blacks has increased to 45.3 percent in 1986 while decreasing to 39.6 percent for whites.[11]

The Willie Horton TV ad reflected this scapegoat mentality just as surely as TV programs historically have made the black man a scapegoat for the nation's vices. Fortunately, change is slowly underway on the nation's airwaves and at the movies. With the inception of "The Cosby Show," a large number of programs are now showing black men as more than the down and out or the criminal type; doctors and lawyers are appearing on television and in the movies. In *The Posse,* moviegoers learn how black men helped settle the West. In the highly acclaimed Civil War epic *Glory,* black men fight for their own freedom and act heroically. Slowly but surely black men are beginning to be seen not as scapegoats in the media; yet a majority of black men still daily combat the insidious effects of poverty, unemployment, and racism.

THE BLACK MAN AS PROVIDER

The black man also must battle unfair treatment in the workplace, a treatment that leaves black males without the means to provide for themselves or their families. This inability to provide deeply hurts the black man's sense of identity.

Women, of course, also are a minority and rarely have received equal treatment with men in terms of job opportunities, pay, and recognition. Still, as George Gilder argues in his book *Sexual Suicide,* "The feminist movement is the greatest enemy to black progress in America. It influentially opposes programs that are crucial to reestablishing the black male as chief provider and supporter of his family."[12]

Please do not misunderstand me. I believe many of the issues of equality and justice that confront women also confront racial minorities. Yet, there is a point where the agendas of each can keep one oppressed while lifting another—give one access, while one is still in survival.

This is clearly evident when an employer is considering the hiring of a new worker. He can satisfy gender and ethnic requirements by hiring a black woman. Affirmative Action classifies women and many ethnic groups as minorities. So by hiring a black or Hispanic woman, he has filled two types of minority requirements with one person. The loss once again is the black man's. This also damages the relationships between black men and women, because black men quantify power in terms of economics. This potential loss of more power can cause tremendous tension in the black community.

A black man perceives his role as provider. Therefore, being unemployed cuts into the heart of his identity and feelings of worth. Researchers Noel Cazenave and George Leon studied middle-class blacks and whites and found that, generally speaking, white middle-class men emphasize the more expressive or egalitarian aspects of their male role (for example, being nurturant and sharing feelings), whereas black middle-class men emphasize more of a traditional approach to their male role (for example, work hard and be a good provider).[13]

But why? Cazenave and Leon have postulated that because white middle-class males occupy a dominant position in society, they have a "majority-maintenance perspective," proving their masculinity largely by maintaining their privileges and keeping the status quo. In some ways, white middle-class males do not have to overextend themselves in traditional ways to prove their manhood (become overachievers at work); thus they can afford to be more expressive and less traditional in their male role behaviors.

On the other hand, black middle-class males seek to attain "a minority status" in performing their male role, Cazenave and Leon argue. As minority members, black men have few privileges; this forces most middle-class black men to work especially hard to attain the highly desired "good life." What white men already have becomes a basic goal for black men. To accomplish this, black men, especially those moving into middle-class, place a high priority on the provider role.[14]

HOW BLACK MEN RESPOND TO THE SCAPEGOAT ROLE

Those are some of the reasons that black men are seen as a scapegoat. How does this affect an African-American man you will meet or know? He will end up fulfilling the role of scapegoat; or he may try his best to overcome the role but in the process will feel he must cover up his blackness. How a black man copes with his feelings has a lot to do with his socioeconomic bracket—those who have supposedly "made it" and those who are still trying to "make it." While the two classes of people share similar feelings, the coping styles concerning these feelings vary according to one's socioeconomic status.

Those Who Have Made It

In his book *The Rage of a Privileged Class,* Ellis Cose listed twelve areas that successful black professionals battle as they continue to endure prejudice as an obstacle to professional respect and recognition. The twelve areas are mentioned in the article, all of which impact men of color:

1. Inability to fit into a white environment
2. Lack of respect
3. Low expectations
4. Shattered hopes
5. Faint praise
6. Coping fatigue
7. Pigeonholing
8. Identity troubles
9. Self-censorship and silence
10. Mendacity
11. Collective guilt
12. Exclusion from the club[15]

Many black men I have interviewed, as well as myself, have experienced most often six of the twelve areas: inability to fit into a white environment, lack of respect, low expectations, identity troubles, self-censorship and silence, and collective guilt.

Let's look at four of these areas to better understand how relatively successful black men cope with racism.

1. *Inability to fit in.* I attended a Midwest seminary in the late seventies, one of three African-Americans on campus; I would become only the fifth American black to graduate from this stalwart evangelical school. One of the criteria for my "making it" was that I become some kind of a cross between E. V. Hill and Tony Evans, two prominent black evangelical pastors. It seemed to me, looking back, that I had to fit a certain profile in order to be acceptable. I had to be articulate, intelligent, and portray the proper etiquette. These standards did not seem to be as rigidly applied to white students.

The unspoken assumption I worked under was that, because I was black, I had to pass the so-called "acculturation" test in order to fit in. In trying to pass the test (and eventually succeeding), I sometimes found myself at odds with fellow African-Americans who did not pass it as well.

2. *Lack of respect.* A second element pressing upon black men who find relative success is the constant sense of having to "perform" or prove oneself as an African-American. Once, standing outside a common campus area at Denver Seminary, I chatted with a colleague, when a senior student approached us. The student, who happened to be white, addressed my colleague as "Dr." and me as "Mr." He did this several times. This student knew I also had a Ph.D. and even had me for a couple of classes but did not accord me the respect of my colleague.

Status is something that constantly needs to be earned by a black man. In *The Rage of a Privileged Class,* Ellis Cose noted:

> Knowing that race can undermine status, African-Americans fre-
> quently take aggressive countermeasures in order to avoid harassment.
> One woman, a Harvard-educated lawyer, carries a Bally bag when go-
> ing to certain exclusive shops. Like a sorceress warding off evil with a
> wand, she holds the bag in front of her to rebuff racial assumptions, in
> the hope that the clerk will take it as proof that she is fit to enter.[16]

Often a black man will dress in fine clothes just to prove that he deserves to be where he is.

3. *Self-censorship and silence.* The African-American man who succeeds often monitors his words and sometimes chooses to say nothing rather than risk misunderstanding or creating offense. I remember the first time I spoke with passion in a faculty meeting. I expressed concern about the lack of minority representation on our campus. I was the *only* minority faculty member and often the only person of color on our campus.

I continued to voice my opinion about this matter on several other occasions. Then someone pointed out to me that maybe I was too "emotional" and perhaps angry. I have since learned that whites do not want a black person to be angry; certainly they do not want him to express that anger. You see, there is a stereotype that if a black man is angry he will lose control. I have since discovered that I hesitate to speak up on racial issues for fear of being typecast as an "angry black man."

Many other black men suffer in silence for fear of this same issue or a similar misunderstanding of the intent of our words or the positive motives behind those words. We are at times under suspicion, probably because other cultures, especially the dominant white one, do not understand us. I have found that black men often fear expressing themselves for fear they will be subject to the stereotype of the "angry black man" or be blamed for others' problems. So, they say nothing or limit what they say.

As a result of stuffing their feelings—which at times do include anger—many black men are in a constant state of anxiety and take it on the chin physically. They often develop high blood pressure, ulcers, or similar stress-related ailments because of having to stuff their emotions even more so than their white counterparts.

4. *Collective guilt.* Political scientist James Q. Wilson has argued that the "best way to reduce racism . . . is to reduce the black crime rate." Wilson revealed the devastating consequences of generalizing by the American public: Many honest and hard-working black men end up being lumped with their brethren who commit crimes. It's a common stereotype: blacks are prone to criminal behavior. Yet crime infects all racial groups, including Caucasians. But blacks of all social classes bear a collective guilt.

A black friend of mine I'll call Pete once went into a store to buy some clothes. The person who waited on him said the store recently had been robbed by some black teenagers. The salesman then castigated Pete, telling him, "Why can't you people get your act together!"

Several years ago a traffic officer pulled me over for driving 5 MPH over the speed limit in Dallas. Before I knew it, he had called four other police cars as back-ups. When I finally exited my car, eight police officers surrounded me, guns drawn. One of them pushed me up against the car.

They discovered I was a seminary student and decided I must be OK and let me go. I am convinced that because I was black they considered me dangerous until I could prove otherwise. I was not treated as an individual but as a generality.

These are the key issues that many black men must face who have supposedly made it. As a result, you will meet many African-Americans who feel isolated and powerless—and angry.

I have found that most "successful" black professional men do several things to cope with the feeling of being not quite good enough. Many times they will compartmentalize themselves. When the black businessman goes to the office, he will have to deny his blackness so that it does not get in the way of his making it up the ladder in the white corporate world. Also, the black man feels he has to "numb out" emotionally so that he does not feel the subtle barbs of racism that come his way.

As a result, many of these "successful" black men feel frustration and resentment but learn not to show it for fear it will get in the way of their advancement.

Those Who Have Not Made it

But what about the ones who have not "made it?" How do they deal with these same issues?

Richard Majors has described a particular coping mechanism that many young black males use who must find an alternative "masculine style" from the one embodied in the dominant middle-class culture's expressions of masculinity. These young adults lack a good-paying job, or else lack success in their work; or they may be unable to buy a home. So they look for another badge of masculine success. Many, especially those in the lower socioeconomic groups, have learned to posture or pose themselves as if to tell everyone else, "Hey, look at me, I am somebody" when the world seems to be saying to them "you are a nobody." Because most black males "mistrust the words and actions of dominant white people," they adopt poses "that connote control, toughness, and detachment," according to Majors. They act "cool," and as Majors explains,

> Being cool is a unique response to adverse social, political and economic conditions. Cool provides control, inner strength, stability and confidence. Being cool, illustrated in its various poses and postures, becomes a very powerful and necessary tool in the black men's constant fight for his soul. The poses and postures of cool guard, preserve and protect his pride, dignity and respect to such an extent that the black male is willing to risk a great deal for it. One black male said it well: "The white man may control everything about me—that is, ex-

cept my pride and dignity. That he can't have. That is mine and mine alone."

The cool pose does have its cost. A black man must always maintain his manly posture for fear that others may think him less than a manly man. He cannot allow himself to be vulnerable because he might be humiliated by others. The problem with the cool pose is that there may be times when such a contrived and controlled posture prevents him from letting down his guard and being "himself."[17]

Also, the cool pose further reinforces the very caricature that white society has of the black man. James Doyle writes in *The Male Experience*:

> Although being cool may provide a black man some protection from the onslaughts of racism, being cool reinforces all of the negative qualities of the dominant white man's super-masculine role. Thus being cool may be a way to show contempt for all of the racist aspects of white society while providing little, if any, relief from the damaging demand of an outmoded view of what being a man means.[18]

What can we do as men of integrity—Christian men—both black and white—to get rid of the "scapegoat" role that many black men feel? If you are a black man, how do you deal with these feelings of inferiority and anger inside? If you are a man of another color, how do you empower your black brother?

Read on, my brother. I have some good news for these bad times.

TAKE ACTION

1. What is your attitude toward black men; do you regard them as scapegoats for problems of crime and injustice? If you are a black man, think of an instance when you experienced prejudice or were made to feel like a scapegoat. How did you feel?

2. If you are a black man, have you ever "denied your blackness" in order to advance? How do you compartmentalize your life? In what ways do you numb your emotions? How do you think Christ views your blackness?

3. If you are not a black man, what is your attitude toward black men expressing angry emotions? In what ways can you as a non-black person change your choice of words and language to show respect to blacks?

CHAPTER THREE
Inside the Hearts of Men of Color

A few years ago a researcher performed an experiment using a certain type of fish and a glass plate. Several carp swam in a tank of very clear water with a large plate of glass dividing the aquarium's middle. The experiment consisted of some food being placed on the other side of the plate glass—food that was very desirable to this type of fish.

Every time the carp tried to reach the food, they did not see the plate glass and swam full speed into it, only to be stopped by the glass. This went on for several days, with the carp eventually "wising up"; they saw the food but no longer tried to reach it. After about a week the plate glass was removed from the tank so that the food would now be accessible to the fish. An interesting phenomenon happened. Every time the carp would head for the food they would stop just short of it and not get the food. Although the plate glass had been removed they still operated as if the glass were there. The carp now had no physical impediments to getting the food they desired, but their past experiences kept them from attaining what was available to them.

The very same phenomenon is true among minority men, especially black men. Often I have heard my white brothers say, "Black people have so many great opportunities today, and yet as a people they seemingly have not progressed very far." I sometimes get the feeling from my white friends that the inferiority of blacks is due to the black person's motivational level. The opportunities are there but blacks do not work hard enough to take advantage of them, they imply.

As a black man, at first I felt anger upon hearing these remarks; now I realize that these comments were made out of a lack of understanding concerning the thoughts and feelings of minority men and, in this case, black men. In this chapter we look inside the hearts and minds of minority men, particularly the black man, to understand several of the barriers they face to manly expression.

THE POWER OF THE PAST

People do not develop in a vacuum. Just as in any family, experiences have given to children either a sense of being accepted and wanted or a sense of being unaccepted, even a burden to the family.

When a child grows up in an environment of acceptance, he typically develops a healthy self-image and confidence. Any child who grows up within a family that has the characteristics of an open system (see chapter 1) will feel strong and whole in terms of social relations, status, and security. For instance, in his social relationships he will view most people as friendly, with whom he can form close personal relationships; as a result he will like and seek close companionship with most others. In his sense of security, he will believe that the world is a safe place that is predictable and free from worry and uncertainties; he also will believe that most people can be trusted.

But what if a child grows up in a closed family system, a system marked by a pervading sense of unacceptability? This environment also would influence a child, but in a notably negative way. Consider the likely outcomes in social relations, status, and security:

Social Relations
1. The world is a hostile, unsociable, closed place.
2. Most people are unfriendly and avoid personal relationships.
3. The child begins to dislike and avoid close companionship with certain others.

Status
1. The world is a competitive place full of prejudice and discrimination, with little opportunity.
2. Most people are not treated with equal fairness and respect, and their strengths and personal worth go unnoticed by others.
3. The child feels little worth and his strengths are unrecognized by others.

48

Security
1. The world is a harmful place that is unpredictable and full of worry and incertitude.
2. Most people cannot be trusted.
3. The child mistrusts and suspects the motives of others.

In American society, dominated by the Euro-American, white majority, most members of minority races feel and often have been treated as though they have been raised in a closed family system. They believe the world is hostile and unsociable, a competitive place full of prejudice and discrimination. They believe that most people cannot be trusted. And they act according to this closed-system viewpoint. In addition, many minority men have grown up in families dominated by a closed system. Thus both society and their families of origin have given them a restricted and negative view of their world.

A SENSE OF SHAME

As a counselor and psychologist, I have found that anybody, regardless of race, who comes from a closed system will have a profound sense of insecurity and inferiority—in essence, a sense of shame. If the family is in disarray, the schools poor, the neighborhood unsafe, then everywhere the individual looks he will see reasons to not trust or not feel trustworthy. In contrast, if his childhood environment is stable and positive, the family whole and loving, the schools good, and the community stable and safe, he will believe in himself and have confidence.

I am not saying that one cannot overcome a difficult childhood, but that a grid is established in childhood as to whether we can approach the world with confidence—a strong self-image—or with shame and doubt—a poor self-image. Depending upon one's experiences, the plate glass will be seen as merely an obstacle to overcome, or as a natural way of life. For many men of color, the plate glass remains an ever-present obstacle.

Shame in the First Grade

My first and thus most significant encounter with insecurity, shame, and doubt took place when I was in the first grade. The teacher had made it clear who was intelligent and who was not; her method was to put each student into one of three reading groups that would show her students' ability or lack thereof. The "owls" were the smartest and could read clearly and precisely on command. The "giraffes" were not as fluent in their reading abilities, but they could get through the reading material with minimal difficulties. Finally there were the "Humpty Dumpties," my group. We were on the wall and off the wall. Some days, when we could overcome our anxieties, we would read pretty well; other days, we could not get through a paragraph.

Along with being in that group, I was also the only black in the class, and the teacher singled me out as the worst among the Humpty Dumpties. She made it clear that "my people" just did not seem to get it. I thank God for a mother who felt I could get it. My mother bought all the reading materials and read with me daily. I did get out of the Humpty Dumpties, though not the giraffes, and was able to pass first grade.

Every man has an innate capacity for insecurity. But our experiences can expand and deepen that tendency to feel insecure. The past experiences of black people as a whole, indeed of most minorities, have ingrained a deepened sense of doubt, shame, and inferiority upon their minds. We feel shame for what we are. People feel *guilt* because they *did* something wrong, but people feel *shame* because they *are* something wrong. Today, even with a Ph.D. degree showing academic mastery of a subject, I still wonder if that is enough to make me believe I have personal worth.

Social Shame

Among black people, social shame has existed for a long time, tracing all the way back to the slave days in the early 1800s. Social shame is when one group is despised and rejected by another group.

When slavery was common in America, shame for blacks was perhaps at its most obvious. A slave was a slave for one major reason: to be systematically shamed by another group. Yes, there were economic reasons as well, but the system that typically subjugated American blacks and made them virtual property without personal rights was in place to create shame and total, ultimate submission.

A typical classified ad in a Southern newspaper in the 1800s read as follows: "Negroes for sale—A Negro woman 24 years of age and two children, one eight and the other three years of age. Said Negroes will be sold separately or together as desired." At the auction, the woman would be placed with the other female slaves and put on the block.

A buyer could inspect her as if she were a horse or a cow. He could force her mouth open to look at her teeth, feel her biceps and thighs and maybe have her take off her clothes to examine her body for lash marks. She would then be sold—possibly separated from her children. If she cried for her children, it mattered little; her shrieks were no different than a pig's squeal.

Lewis Smedes describes the undercurrent of shame that exists when one group denies another its basic human rights:

> When I, in the pride of my group, despise another person simply because she is a member of a group that my group despises, I shame her.... When I will not allow you to have the same rights that I have simply because you belong to a group that I think threatens the privileges of my group, I shame you. I have reduced you; I have turned you into a nonperson with no identity but the name of the group my group despises.[1]

Most minorities endure the stigma of skin color, an easy way for the majority culture to label the minority. And skin color is perhaps most obvious within the black race, since all minorities are being compared against the white-skin majority. The condition of being black in America means that one is likely to endure more wounds to one's self-esteem than others and that the capacity for shame and doubt borne of these wounds will be compounded and expanded by the black race's reputation for inferiority based upon past experiences.

Shelby Steele wrote, "Black skin has more dehumanizing stereotypes associated with it than any other skin color in America, if not the world." The historian has outlined the implications of black skin on both the African-American and the predominantly Euro-American society:

> When a black presents himself in an integrated situation, he knows that his skin alone may bring these stereotypes to life in the minds of those he meets and that he, as an individual, may be diminished by his race before he gets a chance to reveal a single aspect of his personality. By the symbology of color that operates in our culture, black skin accuses him of inferiority. Under the weight of this accusation, a black will most certainly doubt himself on some level and to some degree. The ever vigilant anti-self will grab this racial doubt and mix it into the pool of personal doubt, so that when a black walks into an integrated situation—a largely white college campus, an employment office, a business lunch—he will be vulnerable to an entire realm of his self-doubt before a single word is spoken. This constitutes an intense and lifelong racial vulnerability and anxiety for blacks.... This vulnerability begins for blacks with the recognition that we belong, quite simply, to the most despised race in the human community of races.[2]

ABANDONING THE STEREOTYPES

If you are a non-black, your past family experiences have influenced your attitudes toward blacks. In many cases, non-blacks have not had direct contact with African-Americans. If that's your case, you probably have picked up stereotypes from your family, friends, television, movies, and newspapers. The steroetypes help you classify a group of men you do not know. They also let you lump together people who are unique.

The solution to this unfair generalizing is to get to know African-Americans by spending time with them in different settings. Consider this setting. As a lecturer and seminary representative, I have been able to speak to predominantly white audiences. Most people in the audience are unaware that I am African-American until I make it known. I find it humorous that people have mistaken me for other ethnic groups, such as Jewish, Iranian, Egyptian, or a dark white man.

When I tell people, usually after I have spoken to the group a couple of times, that I am black, the reactions have been interesting. First, they stare in disbelief and then become a little uncomfortable. Yet, this mild anxiety quickly subsides, and we settle into a positive relationship.

What has happened to help them regard me, a black man, positively? Clearly, they were uncomfortable having their stereotype broken. But I believe that they accept me as a person because they have: (1) felt helped by my message, (2) realized that my issues are not that much different than their own, and (3) built some sort of a relationship with me which has been unhindered by stereotyping.

Research has shown that attitudes about other races do not change by legislation but by relationships. It is only through the context of relationships that we will be able to overcome the stereotypes which have kept us apart.

Generally speaking, this is a process and will take time. We must recognize that our cultural experiences are a part of who we are—not all of who we are. Every man shares common human experiences and feelings. All men in our culture, for instance, feel isolated, powerless, and angry. As a result of our culture all men feel confused as to what it means to be a man in today's society.

Second, we must recognize that all men have distinctive, specific cultural experiences. This is where understanding another man's culture will help a man from the majority culture to connect with a minority man and vice versa, because our cultural context (i.e., our past experiences) does influence the way we approach life.

Third, we must also realize that we are relating to an individual —not the total race—whose personal experiences make him one-of-a-kind. Thus we should treat each person as unique.

A black friend of mine from Texas used to become very angry when both whites and blacks would criticize him for not living in the inner city and ministering to "your people." The critics seemed to assume that because he was black he was not fulfilling his calling. They ignored his distinct background, not realizing that he grew up on a farm in West Texas and took care of pigs and cows when growing up. He felt no more comfortable in the inner city than a white person would from suburbia. He felt called to work in academia because of his ability to educate and model to whites that a black man was intelligent and had something to contribute.

If we treat each minority person as an individual, recognize his distinct cultural experience, and yet share the common human experiences, we can begin to form relationships with men from various ethnic backgrounds.

But specifically, what must happen in order to transcend the "scapegoat" stereotype that has kept black men in a place of inferiority and kept white men at a distance? What must each of us do to bring about the healing for reconciliation? It will take effort by every man.

WHAT AFRICAN-AMERICANS CAN DO

I believe African-American men can do four things to start the movement toward reconciliation with the white majority culture. In addition, there are a series of attitudes that black men, indeed all men of color, can do to promote reconciliation with the American majority culture.

1. Achieving Self-acceptance

The experience of being accepted is the beginning of healing for the feeling of being unacceptable. How important is acceptance? As Smedes wrote:

> Being accepted is the single most compelling need of our lives; no human being can be a friend of himself while at the edges of his consciousness he feels a persistent fear that he may not be accepted by others. Not accepted by what others? By anyone important to us who may size us up and find us wanting. Our parents, our colleagues and bosses, our friends, *especially ourselves, and finally our maker and redeemer.*[3] (emphasis added)

One major issue a black man must deal with constantly in his life is a feeling of inferiority. This feeling of inferiority can lead to a pervasive sense of being a victim (the fish and the glass) and not being worthy or constantly having to prove one's worth.

2. Becoming Survivors

As black men, we must see ourselves not as victims but as *survivors*. We must disregard the prevailing victim-focused black identity. Victim-thinking can keep you from seeing the opportunities and thus cause you to stay stuck in anger. It is true that whites must guarantee a free and fair society, but as a black man I must be responsible for pursuing my own life and dreams. I must force myself to focus upon what is left—not what is lost.

We can escape this victim mindset, becoming a survivor, by (1) resting in the grace of God and (2) starting from our present situation, whatever it may be. Why should we rest in God's grace? Because the surest cure for feeling unaccepted as a man is to know that we are accepted by the grace of one whose acceptance of us matters most— the Lord Jesus Christ. Again, Smedes has written,

> To experience grace is to recover our lost inner child. The heart of our inner child is trust. We lose our childhood when we feel that the persons we trusted to accept us do not accept us or that they may reject us if we do things that displease them. Shame cheats us of childhood. Grace gives it back to us.
>
> The trusting child does not have a worry in the world about whether he is smart enough, or handsome enough, whether he has accomplished enough with his life, or been good enough to be acceptable to his parent. He trusts that the someone who holds him, warms him, feeds him, cradles him, and loves him will accept him again and always. . . . Grace overcomes shame, not by uncovering an overlooked cache of excellence in ourselves but simply by accepting us, the whole of us, with no regard to our beauty or ugliness, our virtue or our vices. We are accepted wholesale. Accepted with *no possibility of being rejected. Accepted once and accepted forever. Accepted at the ultimate depth of our being. We are given what we have longed for in every nook and nuance of every relationship.*
>
> We are ready for grace when we are bone tired of our struggle to be worthy and acceptable.[4] (emphasis added)

Resting in the grace of God frees us up, as black men, to not look outward to others for approval, but upward to Him who has approved us. We begin to live life differently because the only thing that matters is what the Lord thinks of us. We no longer buy into being the Scapegoats of society. We are no longer *victims*; we are *victors*.

Accepting myself also means taking responsibility for my present situation and moving forward. In other words, I take responsibility for building a new life out of whatever talents I have been given in whatever circumstances I have been placed. Each of us can only do what we can with what we have been given.

Of course, as African-Americans, doing our best to better our circumstances at times will also require our being prophetic, telling those in the majority about the resources that they must use fairly and equitably. But no white man is responsible for my development as a person—that is up to me.

One of my mentors pointed out to me that he grew up poor physically, but he did not grow up poor mentally. He said, "Being poor is one thing but thinking poor is another." My friend did not think poor. He now serves as the minority affairs director of the graduate school where I received my master's degree in theology.

Once again, by resting in the sovereignty and grace of God we do not waste our energies raging against the what-ifs, but we deal with the what-ares.

3. Forgiving Those Who Shamed Us

The act of forgiving can be difficult, but it is through forgiveness that we can start fresh and truly bring about reconciliation. There are five keys to forgiveness.

1. *Recognize that there are legitimate reasons for being angry.* When I was in seminary, insensitive remarks were made in my presence by white brothers. Some remarks were made out of ignorance and some were meant to put me in my place. Some were sins of omission and some sins of commission. Both hurt deeply. I forgave them —but I also hold them responsible for what they did.

2. *Surrender your right to get even.* Howard Hendricks, distinguished professor at Dallas Theological Seminary, is a key person who influenced my life. I will never forget what he said when I mentioned these racial issues. "Rod, as a black evangelical you will have to learn to laugh a lot because if you do not, you will become angry and bitter at our ignorance in relating to you. We are going to make a lot of mistakes."

I learned to surrender getting even and agreed to live with the score untied. As a black man, you can—and must—do the same, so that Jesus may be honored through your life and that the sin of bitterness has no sway over your life.

3. *Recognize that the person who offended you is human.* Recognize that even though what he or she did was reprehensible, it came from a faulty, depraved human being—much like yourself.

4. *Try to understand why they did what they did.* This may take some time because no reason seems acceptable at first. Slowly, as understanding comes about, you will go from anger to compassion, which leads to the last step.

5. *Accept the person who made you feel unacceptable.* We finally are able to have reconciliation because we offer to the one who shamed us the grace that God has offered us. We now leave the door open to have the relationship God has intended for us to have as brothers.

4. Not Waiting Until the Other Person Changes

Movement cannot depend upon change by the other person. If we blacks wait, then we are once again put into a position of feeling powerless. We can initiate, we can forgive—we need not wait. As one of my professors used to say, "The only person I can be responsible for is my own actions and reactions—what the other person does is up to them."

Other Attitudes and Actions

In addition to the above four steps, there are other attitudes and actions we African-Americans can take to promote reconciliation with our white and brown brothers.

- Recognize that openness is healthy.
- Work with and interact with your white brothers.
- Treat people as individuals.
- Recognize that whites are human beings and have their own hang-ups.
- Show an interest in understanding a white's point of view.
- Acknowledge that there are those whites who want reconciliation.
- Allow whites to experience unaware areas of racism.
- Express your true feelings. If you "stuff" your feelings, you will likely explode in anger at a later time. Express feelings appropriately, of course, but do not deny them.
- Meet whites half-way; be ready to accommodate.
- Treat whites on a one-to-one basis.

- Show pride in your heritage.
- Remember and heed the injunction of James 1:27. Be quick to hear, slow to speak, slow to wrath.

WHAT NON-BLACKS CAN DO

Often I hear my black brothers argue that they are the ones always crossing over to the "white man's turf." They say that it seems that for movement to take place in race relations we blacks must be the ones to make the first move. If reconciliation is to take place there must be movement on both sides.

In order for reconciliation to occur between black men and white men, I offer the following do's and don'ts for non-blacks, especially my white brothers as they cross over to the black man's turf.

Do's and Don'ts

Do Assume:

1. Blacks are human—with individual feelings, aspirations, and attitudes. Sometimes there is a tendency on the part of whites to make generalizations or to say, "Well, you are an exception." No, I am *me*.
2. Blacks have a heritage of which they are proud. Even though the history books do not record many of the accomplishments of blacks, there is much to celebrate. For instance, the cotton gin was invented by a black man, as was the peanut. There are hundreds of accomplishments for which blacks as a people are proud. Recognize them and celebrate them.
3. Blacks are angry. Everyday experiences remind the black man that he is not acceptable. Anger is an ever-present emotion in a black man.
4. Whiteness/blackness is a real difference but not the basis on which to determine behavior. It is true, people are different in skin color, but that is where we must stop. All people have the same needs and desires to live a good life. We must not look at a person's behavior as indicative of an entire race but of that person only.
5. Most blacks can handle whites' authentic behavior and feelings. Blacks value openness and authenticity. Do not try to "identify" by taking on mannerisms of the black person, but be yourself and be open to learn. Be authentic.
6. Blacks want reconciliation. Blacks want harmony to exist in the body of Christ. Reconciliation means we value each other equally. Blacks desire this greatly.

7. As a person, you may be part of the problem. Take time for self-reflection and see if there are any negative attitudes or unhealthy stereotypes that could keep reconciliation from happening.

Do Not Assume:
1. Color is unimportant in interpersonal relationships. It is color that has distinguished a black man as the scapegoat in our society. Just because it has not been an impediment to you does not mean it is not an issue.
2. Blacks will always welcome and appreciate inclusion in white society. Expect to be met with suspicion when you approach a black man. In years past blacks have been included because of guilt and not on their terms. Sometimes blacks have felt included as an afterthought. So there may be resistance.
3. White society is superior to black society. Instead, the two are different. For instance, many blacks are event-oriented rather than time-oriented. Event-oriented individuals usually go somewhere with the attitude "When we get started we start—and we end when we end." In contrast, a time-oriented individual begins and ends with "time" as the issue. Neither perspective is right or wrong—just different. However, if a black man is "late," he is seen as undependable by the majority culture. Instead of judgment, we need acceptance of differences as simply being that—difference in cultural behavior.
4. Blacks are oversensitive. Instead blacks strongly support what they believe. That's how it should be—every man a strong advocate for his position. I have taught in a seminary where most of my students are white. I remember presenting a position on an issue with passion. I was not committed to the position, but I presented it with zeal to stimulate class discussion. No one asked a question for fear they would be shot down. I explained to the class that most blacks come across as advocates for their position. This then gets things out on the table to discuss.

Other Keys for Reconciliation

In addition to the above do's and don'ts, here are eight other positive steps non-blacks can take to open the doors to reconciliation with African-American brothers:

1. Be direct and open in expressing your feelings.

2. If you are white, help other white brothers to understand and confront their feelings.

3. Listen without interrupting.

4. Support self-initiated moves of black brothers, being a coach and cheerleader.

5. Demonstrate interest in learning about a black man's perceptions and culture.

6. Stay with and work through difficult confrontations.

7. Take a risk (being the first to initiate).

8. Assume responsibility for examining your own motives—and admitting what they are.

If we do these things we will experience the truth of Psalm 133:1: "How blessed it is for brothers to dwell together in unity."

TAKE ACTION

1. Do you believe that blacks are inferior? What past experiences influenced this attitude? Would you agree or disagree with Shelby Steele's quote that blacks are the most despised race in the human community of races?

2. Attitudes do not change by legislation but by relationship (p. 52). Using this, reflect on your relationship with God. Is it conducted by legislation or relationship? What about your relationship with blacks or other minorities? What part of your attitude toward minorities can be attributed to common human experience? To specific cultural experience? To individual experience? Is your relationship based largely on legal issues, such as Affirmative Action and housing laws? How does this affect your relationship with them?

3. If you are a black man, can you take the first step toward reconciliation by accepting yourself? Are you a victim or survivor? Read Romans 8:5–38 and Ephesians 2:1–7. How does God view you?

4. If you are a non-black man, can you take the first step toward reconciliation by learning more about the black heritage? By being authentic? Take a moment for reflection. Do you have negative attitudes or stereotypes that keep reconciliation from happening? Read Galatians 3:2–28.

CHAPTER FOUR

The Asian-American Man: The Model Minority?

BY LEONARD TAMURA

W ell, you all look alike to me." Most Asian-Americans have heard the comment, sometimes uttered as an attempt at a joke. Whatever the intent, the phrase has been heard by most Asians in the U.S. countless times. It highlights an important point. Even though as many physical differences exist among Asians as there are within other groups, the misconception persists that Asians are a homogeneous group with few contrasts among themselves. Nothing could be further from the truth.

Many different groups make up the larger category of "Asian" in America: Vietnamese, Japanese, Hmong, Samoan, Chinese, Laotian, Korean, Filipino, to name just a few. Each group differs in its country of origin, language, culture, customs, and sociopolitical history in Asia, as well as its unique history in the United States. To be sure, certain similarities exist, but there are also significant differences between the experiences of a refugee from Vietnam, having just recently arrived in this country, and a fifth-generation Japanese-American who was born and raised in the suburbs of a metropolitan city. In this chapter we will learn to understand better Asian-American men, that is, people who trace their heritage to both the continent of Asia as well as to the Islands of the Pacific.

First and foremost, there is no such thing as a single, unified "Asian-American male perspective." Asian men in America are substantially diverse in their responses, thoughts, and feelings about how they have been treated in this country. Nevertheless, they share commonalities—if not in the ways that they have responded, at least in how Asian-American men have been, and are, treated. Despite the risks of being misunderstood as supporting the inaccurate "you are all alike" mindset, my observations are intended to show their common bonds of Asians and what our Asian brothers bring to the American experience.

ALL IN THE FAMILY

In thinking about what constitutes the "Asian-American role," we must modify slightly the Asian's place in the dysfunctional family system of America, for the Asian-American man does not fill just one single role. As in real families, the roles sometimes change. At different times in this nation's history, in different places, and in different situations, various groups of Asian males have been placed in almost all the roles of Enabler, Hero, Lost Child, Mascot, and Scapegoat. In fact, any one Asian male will most likely have experienced pressure or expectations to fit most of these roles at one time or another in his life. Two roles, however, are the most powerful and frequent: the Hero and the Scapegoat.

The Hero

To many, Asians are the "model minority," an example to be held up as to what can be accomplished in this country "if you really try." This view portrays Asians as hard-working, industrious, and, perhaps most important, compliant. Several accomplishments are cited in support of this view: the economic successes of some Asians and Asian families as each generation (particularly the first) has worked and toiled long hours under difficult conditions to improve the lot of the next generation; the professional successes of some Asians (particularly the later generations) as they have compiled impressive careers as physicians, lawyers, engineers, and so on; and the academic successes of some Asians, particularly in mathematics and science.

The Hero role works well for those who do not wish to acknowledge the ongoing inequality and racism that is entrenched in our society. They can point to the Asians as proof that the United States is an equal opportunity country. This belief in the hero myth is so entrenched that in many, if not most, discussions of racism, as well as in scientific social and psychological studies considering ethnic factors, Asians (and perhaps to an even greater extent, Native Americans) are ignored.

George (not his real name), a friend of mine who used to work in the Colorado state government, told me that when committees were being put together to discuss community concerns, the ethnic groups that were clearly included from the beginning were the African-American and Latino communities. Representation from the Asian- and Native-American communities was often sought hastily and at the last minute, if at all.

Similarly, in a special issue entitled "America's Original Sin: A Study Guide on White Racism," a Christian magazine recently presented several excellent articles on the subject by different authors from many perspectives. However, of the fifty-four articles, not one was from an Asian perspective. It is as if Asians are part of the Anglo culture and not subject to racial prejudice.

In fact, Asians often are presented as having "made it" and held up as an example for other people of color to do the same. "If other groups don't succeed," the proponents of the Asian-as-hero argue, "it must be because they aren't trying hard enough, are too busy complaining, or have some other defect within themselves."

This is unfortunate, because it often pits people of color against each other. It is also unfortunate because it is untrue. The primary problem with depicting Asians as the model minority is that, like most stereotypes, it is too narrow a view. It is not accurate on either end of the success scale.

On the upper end, although Asians are relatively prosperous and successful, they are still not equally represented in the upper echelons. The infamous "glass ceiling" still prohibits progress beyond a certain point. A recent study of Asians in government positions revealed that, whereas Asian-Americans were overrepresented overall in federal government positions, they were underrepresented (less than 1 percent) in the high-level positions known as Executive Service positions.[1]

A reporter for *The Economist* tells this story of race prejudice for a "successful" Asian-American:

> Moon Yuen was a rising star in Bechtel, a leading American engineering company, when he learnt by accident that he would never make it to the top: his job as section head was the limit. . . . Mr. Yuen, like many of his fellow Asians, had bumped his head on the "glass ceiling," the notion, conveniently subscribed to by the white majority, that Asian-American talents flower better in the back room, the laboratory or the classroom than in senior management.[2]

On the lower end, many Asian families are affected by poverty, crime, intergenerational conflict, substance abuse, and more. As *Time* reporter Howard Chua-Eoan wrote in 1990:

> There is no pan-Asian prosperity, just as there is no such thing as an "Asian-American." There are comfortably middle-class, fourth-generation Japanese-Americans, and there are prospering new immigrants from Taiwan and South Korea, all driven by an admirable work ethic. There are also fragmented Filipino families headed by women, and Hmong tribesmen who know little of technology and are dependent upon public assistance. "There are people without hope in the Asian-American community," says Michael Woo, the lone Asian member of the Los Angeles city council. It is a strange notion to those whose only awareness of Asian-Americans is of whiz-kid scholars and hardworking green grocers.[3]

In truth, the various Asian cultures also have pressured Chinese, Korean, Japanese, and other Asians toward financial and social success. We can say parents, in pushing their children to honor the family name, have indirectly fostered the use of the Hero role. Two reasons Asians have worked long and hard to achieve success in America are the group orientation of most Asian cultures and the issue of shame.

U.S. culture stresses the importance of independence and "rugged individualism." Stories abound of self-made men who amassed fortunes by being fiercely independent and doing things their way. From the Revolutionary War to today's army, where men are encouraged to "be all that you can be," Anglos are focused on individual achievement.

Asian culture, on the other hand, generally values group harmony and interdependence over the needs of the individual. The roles in most Asian societies are much more clearly defined, and elders and those in authority are to be feared and respected. In the U.S. the saying is "The squeaky wheel gets the grease," meaning that it is important that you speak up so that your individual needs will be met. In Japan, however, a saying that is roughly translated "The nail that sticks out will be hammered down" means that conformity to the group norm is what is valued (even if it comes at the cost of the individual).

Further, in most Asian cultures, shame is a powerful force. That interacts with the emphasis placed on group, rather than individual, needs so that the individual shuns any action that would cause embarrassment or bring shame on himself or, by extension, his family. This is partly because of the close ties within Asian families and the valuable resources to be found there. It is also due in part to concern not to damage the reputation of the family by letting outsiders know about their problems.

This concern for the reputation of the family extends even to one's country of origin, ethnic group, or culture. There is often an anxiety among Asians that inappropriate actions of any one member will cause the entire group to lose face. When Yoko Ono and John Lennon were in the news during the 1960s, voicing their opposition to the Vietnam War, Yoko's action embarrassed part of the Japanese-American community. The Lennons did many things to emphasize their opposition, including holding a press conference from their bed. The Japanese-American mother of a friend of mine was upset and horrified by their antics. She was very embarrassed by Yoko's behavior and felt that she was bringing shame to all Japanese.

All of these factors—respect for authority and roles, valuing of group harmony, and fear of bringing shame on one's community— have resulted in Asians often tending to downplay or even deny problems, thereby contributing to the image of the Hero role. Although on the surface the picture may be one of success, contentment, or even happiness, that is not always the case. The difficulties, the struggles, and the pain typically are suppressed in order to not speak out of place, not "make waves," or not bring shame to the group.

The Scapegoat

In the role of Scapegoat, Asians are seen as the enemy and blamed for a multitude of problems—economic, social, and political. On February 19, 1942, President Franklin D. Roosevelt signed Executive Order 9066, authorizing the secretary of war to designate "military areas" and exclude "any or all" persons from these areas as a "military necessity." As a result, 110,000 persons of Japanese descent were interned in concentration camps. More than 70,000 of them were American citizens.

The Executive Order was ostensibly to protect national security from the threat of sabotage, espionage, or other subversive activities by those sympathetic to the United States' enemies. A report by Curtis B. Munson, a special representative of the State Department, conducted months earlier and based on extensive investigation, however, had certified the extreme loyalty to the U.S. of the Japanese living in America. But even with this information, President Roosevelt signed the order.

In parts of the United States, citizens expressed their fears that Japanese-Americans within the U.S. would assist their mother country indirectly; local leaders also expressed their prejudice and anger against the Japanese for the devastating raid at Pearl Harbor. U.S. Senator Tom Stewart of Tennessee declared:

> They [the Japanese] are cowardly and immoral. They are different from Americans in every conceivable way, and no Japanese . . . should have the right to claim American citizenship. . . . A Jap is a Jap anywhere you find him, and his taking the oath of allegiance to this country would not help, even if he should be permitted to do so. They do not believe in God and have no respect for an oath.

Although anti-Asian, and specifically anti-Japanese, sentiment reached a high point during World War II, it is once again on the rise. During the period of 1984 to 1990 in Los Angeles County, the number of hate crimes directed at Asians increased 257 percent. A recent U.S. Department of Justice report indicated that there was an increase in hate crimes against Asian-Pacific Americans of 62 percent in a one-year period.[4]

As scapegoats, Asians are blamed for everything from a poor U.S. economy to a person's unemployment. In 1982, Vincent Chin, a Chinese-American, was with some friends celebrating his upcoming wedding when two unemployed autoworkers who mistook him for a Japanese began harassing him, blaming him for their unemployment. Later, when he left the establishment, he was followed by these men, who eventually tracked him down, confronted him, and beat him to death with a baseball bat. They were later acquitted.

A key aspect of this role is that it focuses on and highlights the "differentness" of Asians. Now, obviously, Asians are physically and, to varying degrees, culturally different from non-Asians. The problem with the Scapegoat role, however, is that it takes these underlying truths and exaggerates them to the point where they become insurmountable barriers. Asians are seen as "inscrutable" and from the "mysterious East." This perceived inability to relate to and understand Asians because they are so different, breeds a basic fear—the fear of the unknown.

In 1992 in Baton Rouge, Louisiana, a young Japanese foreign exchange student named Yoshiro Hattori and a friend were trying to find a costume party. Hattori, an avid dancer, was dressed as the actor John Travolta from the film *Saturday Night Fever,* but they inadvertently went to the wrong house. A woman answered the door, saw the Japanese man as someone in fancy clothing and a stranger, and began screaming for her husband. The student went to the side of the house, where he was confronted by the woman's husband, Rodney Peairs. He shouted for Hattori to "freeze." Not understanding English well, Hattori kept moving. Peairs shot and killed Hattori.[5]

Significantly, the news accounts and subsequent trial did not discuss why Peairs's wife began to scream upon seeing Hattori. Apparently no one thought it unusual that she would respond with such intense fear to the seemingly nonthreatening presence of a young Asian man dressed in a disco dance outfit.

Asians in the Media

This representation of Asians as different (and therefore something to be feared) is particularly evident in the media. The vast majority of images of Asian males in the media, particularly in film and television, is extremely stereotyped and one-dimensional. Further, although media depictions of Asians at times highlight primarily the aspect of differentness, at other times the differentness is linked with another element. Frequently that additional element is a portrayal of Asian men as evil and predatory. Another media practice is the ridiculing of Asian men as weak, passive, and unattractive—in short, less than men.

In terms of focusing primarily on the differentness of Asian men, Asian males are quite frequently depicted as foreigners. In these pictures, differences in appearance, dress, or language are often emphasized. Recently, especially in commercials, there have been a lot of images of Asian men either as foreign businessmen or apparent recent immigrants with thick accents.

In the 1993 movie *Falling Down,* Michael Douglas portrayed a white-collar worker who is unable to handle the frustrations encountered by white males in our society. Rita Chaundhry Sethi cites one scene in the movie in which Foster, Michael Douglas's character, has the following exchange with a Korean grocer:

Mr. Lee: Drink eighty-five cent. You pay or go.

Foster: This "fie," I don't understand a "fie." There's a "v" in the word. It's "fie-vah." You don't got "v's" in China?

Mr. Lee: Not Chinese. I'm Korean.

Foster: Whatever, you come to my country, you take my money, you don't even have the grace to learn my language?[6]

Foster then destroys the shop with a baseball bat. (Remember Vincent Chin?) In these scenes we see clearly the focus on the differentness of the grocer with regard to language and accent as well as a portrayal of him as an economic predator with the audacity to charge Foster eight-five cents for a drink.

In considering the addition of the element of evilness, one particular media stereotype that deserves special mention is the ever-present portrayal of the Asian male as the martial arts expert. Again, this focuses on the differentness of Asians and often plays up the mysterious and almost magical powers of the practitioners of martial arts. This might, at first glance, seem at least a more positive image, but in the U.S. media this depiction is almost always linked to the portrayal of the Asians as the "bad guys." They are the drug dealers and the crime bosses.

Guy Aoki, founder of the Media Alert Network for Asian-Americans, describes the typical movie plot this way: "You have a white guy going into an Asian-American community. He knows martial arts better than the Asian guys. He beats [them up]. He falls in love with an Asian woman and takes her away. . . . You have four insults at the same time."[7]

Another example of the portrayal of Asians as evil is their depiction as economic predators. In discussing the interplay between racism and economics, Sethi notes that:

> Racism and economic tension are inextricable because race discrimination against Asians has often been manifested as class competition and vice versa. Since the early 1800s, when Asians became a source of cheap labor for the railroads, we have been an economic threat. . . . Any racial analysis must consider economic scapegoating as an avenue for racial harassment and racial victimization as an excuse for expressing economic tensions.[8]

The third pervasive element in media stereotyping of Asian males is what Tom Kagy, in an article about his experiences as an Asian-American male, describes as the "persistent portrayal of Asian males as homely, comically ineffective geeks."[9] This emasculated picture of Asian men seems to serve the dual purpose of exaggerating supposed differences between Asian and Western males, while at the same time demeaning Asians. Kagy wrote, "No sane adult Asian male could deny that American society seems to find some visceral comfort in making Asian males look bad."[10]

From Hop Sing, the simple, always smiling cook with the thick accent on the television series "Bonanza," to the bookish, wimpy Asian character in the *Revenge of the Nerds* movies, these types of portrayals abound. Representations of Asian men as masculine, attractive, "regular guys" are rarely, if ever, seen.

On a recent comedy awards show, Richard Pryor was given a lifetime achievement award. Eddie Murphy presented the award and made a speech about how much Richard had done to tear down stereotypes and advance the portrayal of African-Americans by moving away from the self-deprecating caricatures like Stepnfetchit, the always smiling, dancing, and rarely speaking black movie character. During the same show a videotape excerpt featured a bit by the comedian "Super" Dave Osborn. In the video, Super Dave, whose cable TV show features parody and broad physical comedy, was assisted by his sidekick, an Asian male named Fuji, who depicted a grossly offensive caricature of an Asian. Fuji was short, wore thick glasses with prominent black rims, had buck teeth, and wore a ridiculous-looking golfing outfit. In essence, he was an Asian Stepnfetchit. Unfortunately, nobody noticed the irony.

SUBTLE RACISM

Through such media portrayals and the lack of daily or personal contact, many non-Asians accepted the stereotypes that Asian-Americans are scapegoats or heroes. The result is a distrust and anger toward Asian-Americans that results in racism, although the racism often is not expressed openly. The negative feelings engendered from viewing Asians as scapegoats often find expression in what might be called the subtle racism that occurs in the words, attitudes, and behaviors of others. These are interactions that occur many times every day.

While in graduate school, the house that my wife and I were renting had some plumbing problems. I went to the local hardware store, a rather small mom-and-pop operation, to buy some parts. I found the items that I wanted and stood at the cash register. The woman behind the register did not serve me but acted as if she were attending to some important business behind the counter. I waited patiently for some time. Finally, another customer, a Caucasian, approached the counter. The woman raised her head, looked right past me, and said to the other person, "May I help you?" Uncomfortably, he pointed out that I had been there first. With an audible heavy sigh, she reluctantly checked me out.

More recently, a friend and I enjoyed a long but exciting day of skiing in Winter Park, Colorado. Afterward we went to the restaurant at the base of the mountain to relax, get some munchies, and wait for the traffic to die down. We started our time outside on the patio, but as the sun went down and it got colder we brought our snacks and drinks inside. We were the only Asians in the room. After a period of time, we finished our drinks and were ready to order again. The waitress, however, seemed to be ignoring us. Parties (of Caucasians) sat down all around us; she took their orders, and eventually served them, all the while walking past us numerous times. She never offered to take an order.

The two incidents I have described may or may not have an underlying racial motivation, and therein lies the problem; sometimes it's hard to tell. In the first encounter, I concluded that racism was the only reasonable explanation for the behavior of the clerk at the hardware store. In the second incident, however, my friend and I finally confronted the waitress regarding our poor service. She explained that since we had glasses on our table that she hadn't brought us, she assumed that we were being served by someone else. This seemed a reasonable explanation and I accepted it. Nevertheless, the entire time that we were waiting to be served, we were wondering what part our race had to do with the apparent poor service. That in itself was draining and difficult.

Carl Bell, a psychiatrist in Chicago who studies racism, calls these incidents "micro-insults" or "micro-aggressions," and it is the often subjective nature of the experiences that makes them so frustrating. As Tom Kagy puts it, "Dealing with the never-ending stream of real or imagined impositions can add up, over weeks, months, years, to a monumental assault on our sense of self."[11]

Such experiences affect Asian men in many ways. Again, individual responses vary greatly, yet the impact is telling. The subtle racism affects Asian men in several areas, including (1) identity, (2) worldview, and (3) constriction or paralysis.

IDENTITY

From the time we are born, we are constantly in the process of developing an image of ourselves. This image includes thoughts, feelings, and beliefs about who we are as men and what our worth is. Our image is influenced by our background, family, social interactions, and so on. All of these experiences provide us with information about how we are regarded and what others, or society, thinks of us. From those experiences our sense of self develops. Ideally, we develop healthy and positive beliefs and feelings about ourselves as Christians, men or women, African-Americans, Asians, European-Americans, Latinos, or Native Americans. These positive views are then hopefully all incorporated into our overall identity.

As we have seen, however, through the roles of Hero and Scapegoat, the messages that an Asian male in this society receives about himself as an Asian are often negative, rigid, narrow, or stereotyped. This can obviously interfere with the incorporation of a positive ethnic identity into his overall view of who he is.

How does this happen? I think many problems occur when Asian men accept and internalize one or the other of the roles (or perhaps, at times, some combination of both).

Interestingly, many Asian men do not admit that they're facing societal pressures and rigid attitudes regarding Asians. They see themselves as masters of their own fate and feel that their success is limited only by their competence and willingness to work hard. In essence, these are men who accept the Hero role and believe it.

The problem is that this view is not always accurate. There are certainly physical, as well as cultural, differences with others in society. Further, as we have seen, the Scapegoat role involves people not viewing everyone as equal. Many incidents, large and small, occur in the lives of Asian men in this country that reinforce the perception that they are neither seen nor treated equally. Those who accept the Hero role, however, essentially deny that this happens. When they are personally confronted with it, it can be confusing and painful.

I remember feeling much pain as a teenager, looking forward to a date with a young lady. My brothers and I had grown up in the suburbs of Los Angeles, and we were among only a handful of Asians in the community and school, which were both populated primarily by whites and Latinos. During this period of time, I thought very little about my "Asianness" and essentially denied (to myself, anyway) that there were any differences between me and my non-Asian friends.

A friend of mine had set me up with a girl from another school; it would be a blind date, as Kathy (not her real name) and I had never met in person. My friend showed each of us pictures of the other, and we were both interested in each other; so we began talking over the phone. We began making plans to meet, but that's as far as it got. During one memorable phone conversation, Kathy told me that she wouldn't be able to go out with me. When I asked her why, she informed me that her parents wouldn't allow her to date a Japanese-American boy. I remember feeling as if I had been slapped in the face.

That incident was, and in some ways still is, a powerful and painful one for me, in part because racism is always difficult to deal with, but also because I wasn't prepared for it. I had essentially denied that I was different. So it was an extreme shock when I was informed that not only was I different but someone didn't accept me because of it.

Some Asians actually accept and internalize the second role. They believe they are scapegoats. I once heard of a young Japanese-American boy growing up in the fifties. Like most boys his age, he spent much of his time playing army with his friends. Part of this play involved him running around with all his friends yelling, "Let's get those Japs!"

The events of my almost-blind date demonstrate how acceptance of the Scapegoat role can occur. The cumulative effect of all the negative messages inherent in the scapegoating of Asians is often an internalized self-hatred or self-reproach. This involves an often unconscious acceptance of the messages promoted by the majority culture.

On the extreme end, at an Asian mental health center where I work as a psychologist, we received a referral for a Chinese-American teenager who, among other things, said that he hated himself (and his parents) for being Asian. The self-hatred is not always that obvious or intense, but it shows up in a variety of ways.

One example might be an Asian's dissatisfaction with his physical appearance because it does not conform to Western European ideals.

Another area revealing the Asian's self reproach can be how one refers to oneself. I know several Japanese-Americans who at times refer to themselves as Japs. Most often this is done in a mocking/joking tone, but I feel that it belies the underlying conflict and seems to indicate at least a partial or unconscious acceptance of the role of Scapegoat.

WORLDVIEW

An Asian's view of his external world, or his *worldview*, is greatly affected by the roles of Hero and Scapegoat, as well as racism in general. The responses seem to lie along a continuum between extreme denial and oversensitivity.

On one end is the Asian man who has accepted and internalized the role of the Hero. This person will tend to downplay or deny the existence of racism. To maintain this worldview, he must continually push incidents of racism out of his awareness.

On the other end of the spectrum is the Asian man who becomes overly sensitive. When he does encounter racism, he goes overboard; receiving a micro-insult, he *always* attributes a racial motivation, even though some of the time it is not there.

Then there are the vast majority of Asian men who are somewhere in between, recognizing to varying degrees the stereotypes but not always sure how to respond. This brings us to our third category.

CONSTRICTION AND PARALYSIS

Among the twelve factors that blacks often struggle with, according to Ellis Cose (see pages 42–45), is self-censorship and silence. For Asian-Americans, a similar struggle takes place, though perhaps in a broader sense. For several reasons, Asian men are not always aware of, willing to talk about, or else respond to being treated in negative or stereotyped ways.

First, they have learned that society in general is usually uncomfortable with discussing racial issues. An African-American friend of mine told me of visiting an elementary school classroom and hearing a child make a racially derogatory remark to him. The teacher responded by putting her finger to her mouth and cautioning the student, "Shhhh!" She did not confront the student or point out the inappropriateness of his behavior. The message instead was "We don't talk about these things."

That seems to demonstrate the general feeling in our society that, if we ignore it, maybe it will go away. But, even if it doesn't go away, at least we won't have to deal with the uncomfortable feelings invoked by racism. Blacks and Asians alike are learning that many still do not want to talk about racial issues.

Second, Asians who want to fit the role of the Hero remain quiet, refusing to complain. As we have seen already, some of the pressures of the Hero role involve minimizing the existence or impact of negative interactions based on race.

Third, Asian culture focuses on group over individual needs. There are prohibitions against making waves or making a scene, and there is great concern over losing face and appearing too sensitive or complaining. Therefore, many Asian-Americans feel constrained to say little, while inwardly they feel they have been slighted or shown injustice.

Finally, the Asian family has a constraining role on the man. Often, probably due at least in part to the experiences of racism by the parents, Asian men grow up with little or no focus on the race issue within the family context. Although she was writing specifically on interracial families, I think what Maria Root has to say on this subject applies also to Asian families in general:

> Unfortunately the stress that has been experienced by ... families, particularly those that have developed during wartime ... has often resulted in a lack of discussion of race, discrimination, and coping strategies for dealing with discriminatory treatment. This silence has perhaps reflected these families' needs for a sanctuary from the painful issue of racial differences.[12]

All of these factors, and probably more, combine to create an enormous pressure toward constriction in the Asian male. This constriction occurs on many levels. First, it involves constricting one's awareness. As we have seen, many pressures to deny or not notice negative or stereotyped treatment exist. Second, the constriction occurs in the area of one's thinking and feeling. It often seems difficult for Asian men to know what to think or how to feel about many interactions. Third, there is a constriction of behavior. The first two difficulties at times lead to a kind of paralysis of inaction and passivity.

The struggle with the second and third levels of constriction are described by Kagy:

> When a passing stranger remarks that it's "nippy out" ... am I being challenged? When I enter a restaurant and find myself being led to a table in a dark corner by the kitchen, am I being discriminated against? ... I suspect most Asian males encounter such incidents every week. What really gets our dander up is the suspicion that some Americans expect to be able to get away with offenses against us, both petty and monstrous, because they believe the stereotype about us—that media-mixed concoction of propaganda, hysteria, and comforting platitudes. Our big challenge lies first in deciding when a racial slight has been intended, then in deciding what to do about it. Here is our dilemma: We want to show that we aren't too meek or submissive to respond to racial slights, but we don't want to overreact where none was intended.[13]

WHAT ASIAN-AMERICAN MEN CAN DO

I strongly agree with Cooper that attitudes about other races are changed by relationships. What, then, are the specific suggestions for healing with regard to the reconciliation of Asian men with their non-Asian brothers?

1. Develop a Positive Ethnic Identity

We are all multifaceted beings. If you are an Asian-American, remember that being Asian is not the sum total of who you are, nor is it your sole defining characteristic, anymore than being male or being a husband does not in and of itself define who a man is. There is certainly a danger in overidentifying with only one aspect of our character. If this aspect is established in anger or opposition to the majority culture, it becomes what Shelby Steele calls a "grievance identity." That is not what I am advocating, and it is clear that this approach is fraught with problems.

On the other hand, a very great price is paid when underidentifying with or denying our Asian heritage and culture—our "Asianness." Although he was addressing the white experience, David Batstone made an important point for everyone:

> From cradle to grave, of course, we are told to feel good, expunge negative thoughts, liberate our shame, love ourselves, and build high self-esteem—all actions of the will that promise to help us reach our full potential as human beings. Certainly, these means to a healthy self-image are, in and of themselves, to be affirmed on our path to affirm life.
>
> But they must never come at the price of denial. Guilt is the debilitating result of repressed memories. Anxiety, neuroses, and even more serious psychological dysfunctions do not derive from mourning, but arise from the fated attempt to hide from historical wounds and to be fed by their destructive power.[14]

I would add that in denying our Asianness, we are hiding not only from the wounds but from ourselves.

But what do we do instead? I think there are three essential steps: (1) becoming aware, (2) accepting ourselves, and (3) integrating our ethnic identity into our overall identity.

Becoming aware of our culture. We must acknowledge and remain aware that, as Asian men in the United States, we each have a unique history and culture. This may seem like a straightforward and obvious point, especially given what I have already said about the majority culture emphasizing our differentness. Yet we sometimes succumb to pressures on us to pretend and act as if we are not different from the majority culture, even though we surely are and need not feel ashamed of those differences.

The task, then, is to acknowledge, in a matter-of-fact way, the very real differences between ourselves and non-Asians. But we need to do this without going to either extreme—not overexaggerating the differences so that there is no common ground, and not denying any differences at all or pretending that they don't exist.

Further, this need for awareness also extends to acknowledging that we endure negative consequences simply because of our ethnic heritage. Scapegoating and racism do exist, not everywhere and all the time, but they are there.

Accepting who we are. Next, as Asian-Americans we must accept, and even value, our uniqueness. The historical myth is that the United States has been a "melting pot," where people from diverse backgrounds can come together to form a new and unique culture. The problem is that this has applied only to Western European cultures. People of color have largely been excluded from this process. When differences have been apparent, there has been an inherent assumption in the superiority and preferability of Western European culture.

Fortunately, there is at least the beginning of a change in this perspective. Stemming from the "melting pot" model, earlier thinking about the adjustment of people coming from non-Western European cultures has focused on the concept of assimilation, of fitting in (which essentially meant abandoning the original culture). More recently, however, there has been a recognition of the ethnocentrism and monoculturalism involved in that viewpoint and a subsequent focus on the value of diversity. Thus, rather than seeing the ethnic aspects of one's identity as something to be shed or hidden, they can become something to be embraced, valued, and even cherished. This can be done without one's ethnicity consuming him and becoming his entire identity.

Integrating Our Ethnic Identity. The final step is to integrate one's positive ethnic identity into the overall identity. Movement away from the concept of assimilation as the ideal has brought with it an understanding of the value of respecting each culture. This is called *biculturalism.* We can retain and even develop a strong sense of our ethnic and cultural identity, while at the same time learning about, valuing, and incorporating into our identity aspects of the Euro-American majority culture that dominates America.

2. *Take Responsibility for Your Own Environment*

Singlehandedly none of us can eliminate racism. What we do have some control over, however, is our immediate environment. Obviously, we all need to pick and choose our battles, and sometimes it is not wise or even safe to get into a confrontation. On the other hand, silence is tacit approval and does nothing to intervene in the perpetuation of the problem.

I would encourage an increasing awareness of the ways that not only Asians but all people of color are subtly and overtly placed in roles, stereotyped, and treated with a lack of respect. With awareness comes a choice of how to respond. This is almost always difficult. Often present is a strong uncomfortableness in dealing with issues of race. The natural tendency, especially for Asians, is to avoid, deny, and pretend we didn't notice.

In most cases, the slights and insensitivities are not malicious or even conscious. But if they are not responded to, they will likely be repeated. I believe our ways of responding should include gentle confrontation and education. The idea is not to get into an argument but to educate one another. It is important to demonstrate that we are all brothers in Christ, and demeaning one group or individual harms us all.

3. Seek Out Opportunities to Engage in Meaningful Dialogue

Once again, racial issues are extremely difficult to talk about. As long as we all engage in the conspiracy of silence, very little, if any, change will occur. We all need to begin talking.

It is important, though, that the talk be real. That means that you will encounter messy, uncomfortable, and negative feelings—on your part and the non-Asian's part. Although this is certainly not an appealing prospect, the alternative is worse; to try having a discussion without acknowledging or addressing the very real and underlying feelings would be just to go through the motions. Neither party would really learn anything of substance about the other, and they would likely wind up more frustrated and distant than when they began. Catherine Meeks makes this point:

> As long as we try to live in this atmosphere of unacknowledged feelings, we create an environment that allows us to be possessed by those feelings. These negative feelings make up part of our personal darkness and become our subconscious shadows. Since all of us have a shadow, it is quite easy to project on to others those qualities which we have refused to face.[15]

WHAT NON-ASIAN MEN CAN DO

Essentially, the advice for the non-Asian man is the same as for the Asian man. It consists of three parts: (1) examining oneself, (2) taking responsibility for one's personal environment, and (3) seeking out relationships within which to engage in meaningful dialogue.

1. Increase Your Self-awareness

Begin to think about the issues that have been mentioned in this book in light of yourself. Try to identify the assumptions underlying your beliefs regarding Asians. You may find that there is a subtle but inherent assumption about the superiority of one culture over another. An openness to this kind of exploration will have a profound impact on your level of sensitivity and understanding.

2. Take Responsibility for Your Own Environment

All the statements made in the previous section above still apply here. One added point is that as a non-Asian, you will likely be subjected to conversation, beliefs, and attitudes that would not come out if an Asian person were present. In these types of situations, the statement "If you are not part of the solution, you are part of the problem" is particularly relevant. Once again, though discretion must be used, silence is tacit approval.

3. Seek Out Opportunities to Engage in Meaningful Dialogue

Again, this advice is the same for Asians and non-Asians. If we are to make any movement toward reconciliation between the races, each of us must take responsibility for reaching out to begin the dialogue.

In closing, I would like to return to the point where I began. In attempting to open a dialogue with an Asian man, it is important to use the information presented here only as a framework and to approach the particular person as an individual. That is just the starting point. Each relationship that you develop and dialogue that you engage in will be a unique and exciting journey.

This is demanding and challenging work. It takes a strong commitment on both sides, but I can assure you that there are non-Asians and Asians alike who are willing and eager to take on the challenge. Try to seek out safe relationships within which to forge new friendships.

TAKE ACTION

1. If you are an Asian man, think of a time when you were silent regarding discrimination. What kinds of micro-insults have you experienced? How did you handle them? How would you handle that experience today?

2. Go over the author's list of media racism again. Do you agree or disagree? What conspiracy of silence exists in the media? Rod Cooper suggested that the portrayal of blacks in the media is getting better. Do you see a movement, either forward or backward, in the portrayal of Asians?

3. As an Asian man, examine the roles of Scapegoat and Hero. Where do they intersect and diverge? For example, if you speak out against the Hero role, are you labeled a Scapegoat? If you succeed because of your hard work, are you seen by others as taking jobs away from "Americans"?

CHAPTER FIVE

The American Indian:
The Invisible Man

BY JEFF KING

A merican Indian men, sometimes called Native Americans or simply Indians, are the invisible men of American culture. As Indians, we are not seen by the larger culture. Yet we are very much a part of this society and have been from the very beginning of U.S. history. American society has made the Indian the "lost child."

Let me introduce myself in an Indian way. Often when Indian people meet, one tells the other what tribe he is and where he is from. Maybe he will also name some of his relatives. The other will respond in kind and ask questions regarding people he may know from that tribe or from that region. This process allows each to "know who the other is." In effect, it is saying, "Now that I know who you are, we can talk." Let me tell you who I am.

I am an enrolled member of the Muscogee (Creek) nation of Oklahoma on my mother's side of the family. My clan is the Potato clan, and most of my relatives are from around Tuckabatchee, which is near Holdenville, Oklahoma. My father was white. My parents met in the army and were married in Korea during the Korean war. My mother did not speak English until she was six years old. She was the one in the family to move away from the home community. The military paid her way through nursing school. I was raised a military kid for most of my growing up years. By the time I was eleven years old I had lived in ten different locations.

However, whenever we were in Oklahoma, we were around my Creek aunts and uncles, so there were cousins and friends to play with. Listening in on conversations in the Creek language—most of which I couldn't understand—I always knew when they were talking about me because they would use the words *Ishti Hecki,* which meant "white boy." I was the child in the family who looked more like my father. It was a cultural joke, and I generally took it as such.

We would also go to stomp dances. These are dances held throughout the summer, usually in remote areas with cleared-out spaces for camps in which certain clans or families lived, ate, and interacted. There are many dances, such as the Green Corn Dance, the Ribbon Dance, the Buffalo Dance, dances that remember certain historic events, and so on. People wear their traditional garb, or just comfortable clothing such as tee shirts and blue jeans.

The dance area is sacred and surrounded by brush arbors, and in the middle is a fire. Traditionally, the fire was brought from the fires of the Creeks' original homeland back in Georgia or Alabama.

The dancing usually begins late in the evening and continues until daybreak. Many women wear leggings that have turtle shells attached to them. The turtle shells have dried beans inside, which when shaken make a beautiful sound. The dance is begun by the male dance leader moving to the fire, followed by several other men. Then the women who have the turtle shells are allowed to join them. After this, others can join in.

The dance leader begins a chant, which is followed by the men responding with a chant. All the while the dancers move in a counterclockwise motion around the fire in several concentric circles. The chants, the rhythm, the sound of the feet on the earth, the drumming, and the shells all combine to carry participants and spectators alike up into the dance of the people.

When I was a kid, I usually was on the outside circle. With my little legs, I really couldn't dance but had to jog just in order to keep up! Just recently I attended a stomp dance in eastern Oklahoma. I danced with my mother and with my son. Three generations of my family connecting in a dance of our culture was deeply moving to me.

I am now a psychologist and part of my work is concerned with the Indian community in Denver. Through this involvement I have found that my mother, my relatives, and the Creek community have passed on to me much more of the culture than I had previously realized. I am deeply thankful for this.

In writing this chapter, I speak from my own experience as an American Indian. I do not claim to represent all American Indian males, and I acknowledge that there are as many differences between Indian men as there are between Indian and non-Indian men. However, I believe that the following information should help you begin to understand the American Indian male experience.

WHO ARE THE INDIANS?

Many people wonder about the proper terminology for referring to the American Indians. Should it be *Native American, American Indian, Indian, indigenous peoples,* or something else? This has not been fully resolved. I prefer American Indian because many non-Indians view Native American as meaning that our people have lived in America for only several generations. I will use the shorter term *Indian,* which most of my Indian brothers and I use among ourselves. For non-Indians, I would recommend using *American Indian* until one feels accepted and comfortable among Indian acquaintances.

When speaking of American Indians, many people do not realize the great diversity existing among tribes. There are more than five hundred federally recognized tribes, plus more than fifty other tribal entities that have not received official recognition. Among the tribes, almost one hundred fifty different languages are spoken, and religious beliefs vary greatly. Nearly half of the Indian population now lives in urban areas. Many still live on reservations that are usually located in remote settings. However, some reservation lands contain towns and cities occupied by Indians and non-Indians alike. Some Indian people live in small towns and rural areas. Regardless of location, tribes still share many commonalities, as we shall see shortly.

A BRIEF HISTORY

In order to talk about issues related to the American Indian male experience, we must first talk history. Here we find the crucial bridge to understanding Indian culture and to crossing the gap between Indian men and other minorities and especially between Indian and white men.

Most tribes share a similar history. More specifically, they share the experience of oppression and other mistreatment at the hands of whites. As I recount the story, remember as pointed out in chapter 2 that the past shapes the present—in this case the personalities and worldviews of Indian men, women, and children. The inequities shown in the past must be addressed by the broader society if true healing among the people of this nation is to occur.

Both the public schools and society in general have described America as the promised land to the early settlers, much as Joshua and the Israelites properly saw Canaan as the Promised Land. And in a sense, America was a promised land, offering religious freedom and economic challenge, while holding untapped riches and resources for the hundreds of thousands who came. However, in this picture the American Indian was labeled the "heathen," or "savage," much like the enemies of Israel who inhabited the lands they were to occupy based on the promises of God.

Thus, within this erroneous view the taking of the land from these people was justified, and the wrongdoings that were committed were excused. All was interpreted in the light of Manifest Destiny— God designed the land for the pioneers, who were destined to unsettle "savage" Indians from the land.

Broken Treaties, Lost Land

Some attempts were made at being fair. Treaties between the United States government and tribes were established. In fact, a major distinguishing factor among ethnic minorities in the United States is that American Indians are the only ethnic minority group whose relationship with the government is on the basis of treaties.

The treaties were violated, however. As Vine Deloria writes, then-President Richard Nixon once warned the American people about the Soviet Union, saying the Soviet leaders and people were bad because they had not kept any of the treaties they had made with the United States. Deloria notes that Nixon made the charge while failing to acknowledge that the United Stated had broken more than four hundred treaties with Indian tribes. Deloria exclaims that at that rate "it would take Russia another century to make and break as many treaties as the United States has already violated."[1] Land was taken via treaty, trade, war, or encroachment.

Not long ago, my children were watching a TV series about Davy Crockett. I felt it important to talk to them about why the Indians were fighting. "How would it feel," I asked, "if someone came to the place where you and your kin had lived for hundreds of years and told you to move out because they wanted it? How would it feel if they showed no respect for you or your people?"

My kids were kind of startled to think about it in that way. They began asking questions as to why they wanted to take the land. One of my sons asked, "Dad, did Davy Crockett fight people from our tribe?"

Many tribes have stories of the sad, long walks their people had to endure as they were forced off their homeland and made to live in areas that others did not care for—often thousands of miles away. President Andrew Jackson, for instance, informed Indian people that the United States government was powerless to interfere with state laws, many of which were forcing tribes to relocate. Georgia and Alabama made it illegal for an Indian to testify in court against a white man, thus allowing white men to perpetrate criminal activities without Indians testifying against them. Jackson recommended removal legislation, and it was enacted in 1830.

Thousands of Indian people were then forced to leave their homelands. Many died en route to a land that no one else wanted. In essence, the federal government stripped tribes of their traditional sources of livelihood and caused Indian families to become more and more dependent on the government.[2]

Indian men were in a bind. They wanted to defend their land and their families. But they also realized that the enemy was too formidable. Their choice was either to fight back and perhaps lose everything, including family, or surrender, which meant accepting relocation and, consequently, a sense of powerlessness. The role for the Indian male was being undermined by these powerful circumstances.

At the same time, educational efforts were underway for the Indian. As early as the 1600s, attempts were made to "educate" the American Indian. Most, if not all, of the early attempts were for religious reasons. The goal of these educators was to get the Indians to convert to Christianity. Jesuits were among the first to try, working with tribes along the East Coast. Franciscans made attempts with many of the Southwestern tribes. Protestants established schools for educating Indians as early as 1627.[3] These approaches were typically white-European styles of teaching with little or no sensitivity to Indian ways of life. Consequently, they were largely unsuccessful in both educating and converting the Indian.

The Boarding School Saga

In the late 1800s the federal government set up boarding schools as the means for educating the Indian people. To understand the tone of this intervention, I quote Fuchs and Havighurst:

> The package deal that accompanied literacy included continuing efforts to "civilize the natives." Old abandoned army forts were converted into boarding schools, children were removed—sometimes forcibly—long distances from their homes, the use of Indian languages by children

was forbidden under the threat of corporal punishment, students were boarded out to White families during vacation times, and native religions were suppressed. These practices were rationalized by the notion that the removal from the influence of home and tribe was the most effective means of preparing the Indian child to become an American.[4]

The first Navajo boarding school charter (in the 1890s) had as its major purpose "to remove the Navajo child from the influence of its savage parents."[5] Another part of this process involved giving the child a new and "proper name," a uniform, cutting short the long hair of the boys, and communicating to these children in numerous other ways that the Indian way was bad and the white way was good.

Imagine yourself as an Indian child going through this experience. What might you begin thinking about yourself, your family, and your people? For most Indian children, there was deep sadness and a sense of loss. Children had an inner battle over the worth of their culture, their parents, and themselves. Most Indian children had to fight, often unsuccessfully, a feeling of hopelessness.

After generations of these "educational procedures," parents came to expect it and allowed it—not because they did not wish for their children to be at home but because they felt powerless to do anything else. As these children became parents, they had no parental memories or patterns to follow in their own child-rearing practices.[6]

The structure of the Indian family was being eroded, affecting both the family and the children. The federal government strongly enforced this "process of assimilation" until the 1920s; after this, the emphasis on assimilation lessened somewhat. For instance, though boarding school attendance was still mandatory, some attempts were made to allow children to attend close to their homes. In the late 1950s the government and their educators began allowing children to remain in their home settings.[7] However, many of the underlying notions of assimilation continue to form the educational system's goals for American Indian children today. Could this be one of the reasons that, among minority groups, American Indians have the highest dropout rates in both high school and college?[8]

PERSONAL HISTORIES

I would like to share personal stories from family and friends. Once, when my mother was in elementary school, her teacher beat her with a cane for missing a math problem. "The only reason I could figure why this happened was because I was an Indian," she told me. There was no one she could tell who could do anything about it.

Sometimes the racism was more obvious. As a child, one of my friends lived on an Indian reservation with other Indian children and enjoyed swimming in the local town pool until a certain time of the day, when all the Indian children had to leave. Out of the pool they came; as they left, the pool was drained. New water was added and the white children had the pool the rest of the afternoon. The woman spoke with anger as she recalled an event that happened more than thirty years earlier, the hurt still present.

More recently, my seven-year-old son reminded me of the ignorance most people have of Indian history and the inaccurate stereotypes many minorities endure. One November afternoon he returned from school with a Thanksgiving handout. He showed me the paper. One side had a game in which the student-player advanced across spaces to his destination; each space had a difficulty or reward that could help or hinder your journey. Of course, the player was a pilgrim, and certain spaces depicted what appeared to be several Indians with bows and arrows about to attack the Pilgrims. These spaces were labeled "Indian raid—jump forward three spaces." The Indians were portrayed as menacing and savage, which is quite the opposite of the spirit of the first Thanksgiving, where Indian and Pilgrim celebrated the harvest together.

The other side of the handout contained a picture of Pilgrims and Indians. It also had pictures of houses and tepees. It stated that the Pilgrims and Indians celebrated Thanksgiving together, and following this "the Indians went back to their tepees and the Pilgrims went back to their houses." A seemingly harmless handout—yet loaded with inaccuracies and prejudice.

First, the pictures of the Indians did not at all represent the Wampanoag tribe that helped save the Pilgrims that first Thanksgiving time. Second, the Wampanoags did not live in tepees. Plains tribes lived in tepees; most Northeastern tribes lived in longhouses or similar structures. Third, why depict Indians with tomahawks terrorizing the Pilgrims? The handout perpetuated a negative stereotype of Indians and neglected to pay any attention to the tribe's dress, housing, or tradition during that first Thanksgiving. Imagine yourself once again as an Indian child receiving this handout and taking it home to your family.

Behind such stereotypes of the savage American Indian man, the Indian seems to be invisible. He goes unnoticed or lightly regarded. Using the family analogy, he has been ignored—the lost child, as we shall see shortly.

Contrast this invisible man with the true Indian heritage. Traditionally, the male role was to hunt or gather, to be the warrior, to be brave, to be wise. These were the channels of manhood for males. Through contact with white society these roles were stripped away and replaced with powerless, dependent roles, or roles that require assimilating to white society and relinquishing one's Indianness.

MEDIA INDIANS

Reminders of this process are portrayed through television, movies, and other media. Have you ever seen a movie about the Indians in which they were the heroes? Even when tribes are portrayed in a favorable light, it usually includes a white man becoming the hero and saving the tribe. Two examples are the movies *Dances with Wolves* and *A Man Called Horse*. Here, Kevin Costner and Richard Harris are portrayed as vital to the success of the Indians.

Most of the movie and television portrayals show the Indian as the savage. In fact, many of my Indian friends remember that when they were children they wanted to be cowboys when playing cowboys and Indians. The stigma—even for Indian children—was that Indians were the bad guys.

Movies and TV programs also depict Indian men as stupid. They are outfoxed by the clever white hero. They also never manage to speak English fluently. Even today when a child wants to imitate being an Indian, he speaks in this broken English: "Me um want food." This type of talk gives a sense of simple-mindedness that belies an Indian's sharp thinking.

Indians are portrayed as heathen, as drunken wild men, and as blood-thirsty renegades. If they befriend the white man, they are his right-hand men—sort of like a servant: Tonto in "The Lone Ranger," Mingo in "Davy Crockett," and Chingachgook in *The Last of the Mohicans* are classic examples.

Recently television writers and executives have begun to present Indians in a more favorable light. The highly rated CBS program "Dr. Quinn: Medicine Woman" features a wise chieftain, Black Kettle (based on the historical figure), and other Cheyennes, including Cloud Dancing, who seeks justice and peace for his people and shows compassion toward all. On "Walker, Texas Ranger," Cordell Walker, himself part Indian, owes much to his Indian uncle, who raised him after Walker's parents were killed in an accident. And the Apache leader Geronimo received an in-depth profile that belied his savage stereotype in a recent cable TV movie on TNT.

Even though these positive portrayals exist, the Indian remains relegated to a supporting role on such televised dramas. The occasional exceptions are some excellent TV documentary specials: "How the West Was Lost," an historical presentation of truces in the U.S.; "In the White Man's Way," a look at Indian boarding schools and education; and "The Native Americans," a realistic portrayal of different tribes.

A STRONG CULTURE

In spite of all the oppression and prejudices, American Indian people have not become extinct. They have survived and maintained much of their culture. This suggests the incredible cultural strength of the tribes. There are many examples of Indian people who have become successful in the white man's world. From Super Bowl quarterbacks Jim Plunkett and Bart Starr to writer/humorist Will Rogers, Pulitzer Prize writer Scott Momaday, politician Ben Nighthorse Campbell, and to many other psychologists, physicians, and businessmen—successful Native-Americans exist in all walks of life. The national high school chess championship was recently won by a school on the Navajo reservation in Arizona. These examples are more remarkable considering that educational provisions for American Indians are among the poorest in the United States.

ADAPTING TO WHITE SOCIETY

In order to be successful, Indian males had to become like white men. They had to think, talk, and act like white men. That is not unlike what the black and Hispanic men face (as Cooper and Miranda note in other chapters). Imagine what effects upon self-esteem and dignity this has had.

Indians have tried to adapt to white society while maintaining their own identity with varying degrees of success. Sociologists call the process of change a person undergoes due to contact with another culture *acculturation*. Though the process is complex, Indians (as well as other minorities) have displayed any of four general types of responses to white society.

First, an Indian may become assimilated. With *assimilation,* the individual rejects the values and ways of his or her own culture and ascribes to those of the other culture. As I mentioned earlier, assimilation appears to be the underlying condition for educational and economic success in America. Often, an assimilated Indian is called an apple—red on the outside but white on the inside. A second response might be *rejection*. This is where he chooses to remain traditional and reject white culture. Third, he may adjust to and live effectively within both cultures, called *biculturalism*. Fourth, he may disown his own culture and not accept the other either. This is called *deculturation*. In a sense, he is a man without a culture and perhaps without an identity.

These positions are not static. Rather, they are fluid and much more complicated than I have described. They may change due to life situations, life stages, and time.

In my own life, I believe I was fairly assimilated, since I grew up in the military rather than in an Indian community. As is true for many Indian men of my generation, our parents chose not to pass on the language or the culture. Our parents were taught in boarding schools that the Indian way was bad. In addition, they wanted to protect their children from having the severe prejudice and discrimination they endured. My mother told me that she didn't pass on the culture because she didn't want her kids to go through what she had to go through.

Even in an assimilated state I knew I was Indian and accepted that. The Indianness began emerging when I went to college to study psychology. It has continued to grow, and I believe I am more able to live in both worlds now.

I have seen bicultural individuals move more into traditional ways. I have seen some Indian people who do not want to acknowledge their heritage. There are many complex reasons for the shifts one makes in their ethnic identification, and it is not for us to judge. However, once you, the reader, realize that this is a process that most, if not all, Indian people encounter you will increase your sensitivity to the culture and allow more room for compassion and understanding, as the Lord has commanded us.

Unfortunately, white people have not been sensitive, even many Christians. Past missionary efforts focused mainly on assimilating the Indian. As late as 1958, more than one-third of the white Protestant and 45 percent of Catholic missionaries among the Indians advocated complete assimilation. Thus, the thinking is perpetuated among Indians that to become a Christian is to become a white man and give up your cultural heritage.

THE INDIVIDUAL VS. THE GROUP

How do American Indians view people and events differently than non-Indians, especially those in the dominant white culture? Indian societies and white societies differ in some fundamental ways.

The Euro-American society in the United States exhibits individualistic values, whereas Native societies are based mainly on collectivistic values and principles. As an individualistic society, America values the individual over the group. Thus, in the U.S. we value the "rugged individual" —the person who can make it on his own; we value self-sufficiency, independence, autonomy, and self-achievement. Most Americans value individual control, competition, and the self-made man.

Different Values

Different values direct collectivist societies, wherein the group is more important than the individual. The person who succeeds in a collectivist society is one who does not put himself forward but, rather, stays with the group. He acts interdependently, cooperates rather than competes, and values the success of the group over his own personal success.

These are the values of the American Indian. The contrast between the dominant American culture and the American Indian minority are pronounced in terms of the esteemed personality traits.

Superior, Inferior

Each style has its merits. Each style works best within its own culture. However, because our own culture socializes us to think and behave within these domains, we usually assume that other styles of living are inferior. If you value individualistic styles of living, then dependency seems a weakness. If you value a collectivist way of life, then, in your thinking, the independent person appears selfish and rude. We need to get beyond these preconceptions and perceptions that being different is being inferior if we are to truly live as brothers. Indians must respect the individual emphasis of his white and African-American brothers; but they must respect the group focus of the Indian, Hispanic, and Asian brother. This requires work—work on ourselves and work to gain more understanding of each other.

Historically, white society has seen itself as superior to people of color; it still does. Whites have expected people of color to come around to their way of thinking and living (assimilation). Thus, very little effort has gone into trying to understand the world of minorities. Even our American history books begin the history of Indians at the standpoint of when whites came into contact with them, disregarding prior history and culture. All of this has communicated a clear message to the Indian: We really don't care about you; we are not interested in you or your culture.

THE INDIAN AS A LOST CHILD

As stated earlier, Indian men have had their traditional roles removed from them. They can no longer be the warrior in the old ways. They can no longer hunt and convey the incredible wealth of knowledge acquired in hunting, identifying plants, knowing the ways of the animals, or imparting the moral wisdom of tribal living.

These roles have not been adequately replaced for the Indian male. For the most part, they have been ascribed roles originated in white society. They must take on the role of the white man. This can be a humiliating position, and historically it has been. Many Indian men have found the warrior role in the military. Military veterans are highly regarded by tribal members. However, the fact that the traditional ways were taken away has not been noticed by society. If this "lost child" were given attention, perhaps action would be taken on the part of society to address these particular needs.

The response by many Indian males is to feel frustrated, and the only retreat available is to withdraw unto themselves. Though a part of the American family, they feel unimportant. And as we have seen, at times they are virtually invisible, ignored by the dominant white culture. As noted in chapter 1, "The quiet, lonely child can remain almost invisible and is treated as such."

Frustration and Confusion

Living in the white man's world involves managing multiple roles, skills, and behaviors. The "lost child" Indian would like some recognition by white American culture. Yet he realizes there is little to no support for his efforts. The "lost child" must also battle the Indian stereotypes placed on him.

The two primary stereotypes are actually opposites. Some view him as the "drunken Indian," who can never amount to anything; others stereotype him as the "noble savage," who represents virtue and harmony with nature. But the truth about stereotypes is that they keep us from seeing the real individual. Stereotyping is a way of hiding from someone who is different from yourself. If the Indian male somehow manages to avoid the stereotypes, he is typically seen as the exception.

Maintaining His Identity

Attempts at becoming part of the family while retaining his cultural heritage have been frustrated. Many Indian men have gone into the white man's world and become "successful," but others have not.

Many successful Indian men continue to embrace their culture and apply their knowledge and success to helping other Indians. Some have viewed the role of the warrior as one that now means to become educated and to use the weapons of white society to fight a different battle, but still involving the survival and well-being of Indian people.

Many Indian males battle to maintain their cultural heritage. This is difficult because that role is not clearly defined these days. There is a continual struggle for many Indian males as to what preserving the culture means. *Does it mean thinking the same way as my elders?* he asks himself. *Does it mean practicing my tribal ways? Does it mean not accepting the values of the dominant society?* Working out this struggle is made even more difficult when the journey is not supported by the broader society. Indian men who are wrestling with these issues should be highly respected for their courage and commitment to their tribes.

A HEALTHY VIEW OF THE LOST CHILD

As part of my private practice, I conduct family therapy. Often parents will bring in their teenage son and essentially say, "Fix him!" During the course of therapy it becomes more and more apparent that the parents have significant problems. They are usually too involved or too uninvolved in the family. Either way, most of the time the parents are not really listening to their son (he is invisible). He has no recourse in terms of voicing his needs, his own thoughts, because they have never been heard. Thus, unconsciously he acts out in various ways—running away, disobeying the rules, or getting in trouble at school.

I have come to view this behavior as pointing to a strength within the family. Often I begin to see the teenager as the healthiest one in the family. He is the only one who seems to recognize the family dysfunction. He may not be able to articulate it, but through his behavior he is calling attention to the problem. I see this behavior as strength because I ask myself, *What if the young man did not protest? What if he went along with whatever mom and dad said? What if he just accepted that poor relationships existed in his family and needs went unmet?* My bet is that he would lose his spirit—that part of him that makes him uniquely him, that makes him feel alive. He must fight; he must reach out somehow. But the channels for healthy communication are absent. Therefore he acts out. I see it as healthy—relatively speaking. It is also usually self-destructive, and, if it continues, it does destroy. But if it has its desired effect, change occurs within the family, and, if not, at least he has kept his spirit alive.

Similarly, most American Indian males feel a sense of not belonging, because they believe (correctly, in my opinion) that the larger society has not listened to their needs or their thoughts. They have been relegated to the invisible. This is not an excuse from personal responsibility but, rather, a framework for understanding these issues.

WHAT INDIANS CAN DO

A number of years ago I was thinking about all the oppression and atrocities brought upon Indian people. From a human point of view, it seemed logical for an Indian person to feel hatred toward the white man. However, for reconciliation to take place, the Indian must be willing to forgive. Models of such reconciliation appear in various stories. My favorite involves John Perkins, a black Christian who now publishes *Urban Family* magazine.

During his ministry in the South as president of Mendenhall Ministries, he was jailed without any charges being filed against him. He relates how the white sheriff "began to beat me, and from that time on they continued beating me. I was just beat to the floor and just punched and really beaten." It got worse as the night wore on. "One officer brought a fork over to me and said, 'Do you see this?'" And he jammed it up my nose. Then he crammed it down my throat. They beat me to the ground again and stomped on me."[9]

John Perkins continued in his ministry, but anger and bitterness ate at him from the inside. Some time later he wound up in the hospital and flat on his back because of overexertion and stress. He said it was at that time that God confronted him with his anger.

> The Spirit of God worked on me as I lay in that bed. An image formed in my mind—the image of a cross, of Christ on the cross. This Jesus knew what I had suffered. He understood. He cared. Because he had gone through it all Himself. . . . His enemies hated, but He forgave. God wouldn't let me escape that. He showed me that however unjustly I had been treated, in my bitterness and hatred I was just as sinful as those who had beaten me. And I needed forgiveness for my bitterness. . . . As I prayed, the faces of those policemen passed before me one by one, and I forgave each one. . . . I could sense God was healing all those wounds that had kept me from loving Whites. How sweet God's forgiveness and healing was![10]

This example, more than any other, has stuck with me. True forgiveness and healing must occur first in our hearts. That is the responsibility of all men—Indian, white, black, Asian, whomever. We must all come to the cross and embrace deeply the love and forgiveness offered there and then offer it to others.

As I stated earlier, the earthly, logical conclusion of most Indian men for past injustices is to hate the white man. However, the noble and humble response is to forgive. Forgiving is the demand Jesus makes on everyone—to forgive those who unfairly malign us, even as Jesus forgave those who wrongly persecuted Him.

Second, we must work through feelings of bitterness. It is amazing to me to read what different Indian leaders such as Black Elk, Red Cloud, and others have said. Their speeches contain no bitterness or hatred. Sadness, disappointment, and anger often are there, but not the bitterness. Many of these men were not Christians, yet they realized the self-injury of bitterness, and they provide a role model for us.

Probably the most difficult task for us as Indian men is to address the issues of discrimination, prejudice, inequity, ignorance, and oppression without becoming like those we oppose. We must guard our hearts from attitudes of hatred, superiority, and revenge. The most natural response to oppression is to oppress back. Spiritually, we must cultivate our hearts; that is, we must seek the Creator for tenderness of heart. At the same time, we need to pray for wisdom in bringing about change, grace to preserve our tribal cultures, knowledge of how to integrate our Christianity and our culture. This requires a willingness to sit down with your white, black, brown, and yellow brothers to pursue peace (Psalm 34:11–14). You and I must cultivate an attitude that trusts a faithful Creator who will right all wrongs and execute righteous judgment throughout the earth (1 Peter 2:23; 4:17–19). We must find in Christ a strength to forgive.

WHAT NON-INDIANS CAN DO

After Cain had murdered his brother Abel, God came to him and asked where Abel was. Cain replied, "I do not know. Am I my brother's keeper?" Then God said, "What have you done? The voice of your brother's blood is crying to Me from the ground" (Genesis 4:9–10 NASB). Yes, we are our brother's keeper. Non-Indians must be involved in reconciliation, and this will mean active involvement. Here are several truths to remember in reaching out to our American Indian brothers. The truths will remind you of the contrasts between Indian and Euro-American culture.

First, remember that American Indian societies are a collective structure, whereas the structure for white society is an individualistic one.

Second, Indian mannerisms differ from non-Indian mannerisms. Our mannerisms, or cultural ways, are formed by worldview; for an Indian, the role of man traditionally is to live in harmony with nature. For most Americans, the role of man is the mastery of nature. The contrast, of course, is great, resulting in significantly different outcomes in one's thoughts, perceptions, and behaviors. To live in harmony for the Indian also means that one lives in harmony with the group. Cooperation rather than competition is emphasized.

How will that affect your interactions with Indians? You will see that they do not necessarily seek to be first or superior; they want everyone to win. Thus, they are great team players. They understand the value of cooperation, and we should appreciate the attitude. One school teacher in Minnesota remarked, "It's really incredible, but when I have Indian students at the chalkboard to compute a math problem, they all finish at the same time!" Billy Mills, the Olympic gold medal winner in track, used to slow down so that the second place runner would not feel humiliated.

In white culture the emphasis is on self-sufficiency, autonomy, and self-control. In Indian culture what is emphasized is interdependency, being a part of the group, and allowing others' input into your decision making. Accept those attitudes among your Indian brothers for the strengths they are.

We need to recognize, however, that there are many exceptions to these behaviors and belief systems. You may belong to white culture and see more of your own style in the Indian category or vice versa. The main point here is that these behaviors are appropriate for their cultural context.

Third, recognize that time is *not* of the essence to the Indian man. The Indian views time as the black and Hispanic view time, and this confuses and frustrates the white man. Many Indian (and black and Hispanic) people are event-oriented rather than time-oriented. Timeliness is not expected of the other, and being "late" is not much of an issue. That's because people matter, and, once with you, an Indian will spend as much time as needed, even delaying an appointment.

One time a Navajo woman and her family planned to stay at our home while conducting business here in Denver. On Monday, which is when they were expected to arrive, my wife fixed a big meal for them. However, they did not arrive until Friday. This was disappointing to my wife, who is white (and time-oriented). For Indian people, however, this would be taken in stride, not seen as a broken promise or as anything out of the ordinary. Time is not a big issue for Native people.

Some of you may be saying to yourselves, *But they should be considerate of those to whom being on time is important.* This is true also. We must all work together to meet each other as we move toward each other in understanding and love. Historically, however, it has almost always been that the Indian must meet the white person on white terms. Rarely has it occurred to him to meet the Indian on Indian terms.

Fourth, recognize that sins have been perpetuated against the Indians, and, where appropriate, ask for forgiveness. Although you may not have engaged in acts of racism and inequity against Indians as a white person, accept ownership of the actions by your white brothers. "I wasn't the guy who took the land and did all those atrocities," you may reply. But even though it wasn't you, it sounds as though you are saying, "I don't accept any responsibility for what has happened to Indian people." But if you do not, I wonder who will.

Earlier, I mentioned the common viewpoint among Christians of seeing America as the promised land, similar to Israel and its promised land. I believe this is an erroneous application of Scripture. I believe a healthier point of view toward the American Indian experience is described in 2 Samuel 21, where the Lord made known to King David that Saul had broken a treaty Israel had with the Gibeonites and had severely mistreated them. This had never been made right. David's godly response was to go to the Gibeonites and say, "What should I do for you? And how can I make atonement that you may bless the inheritance of the Lord?" (v. 3).

Exemplified in this passage is an attitude: taking personal responsibility for reconciliation, even for events not caused by oneself. I believe this is what is necessary for true reconciliation across cultures. In the case of King David with the Gibeonites, he could have said, "It was Saul, not me, who did these horrible things." Rather, he accepted responsibility for a wrong not resolved. I would like to see those in leadership (as well as others) take a responsibility for the inequities that continue for Indians throughout this nation. Yes, forgiveness through Christ has been provided for these past actions. Yet the wrongs still need to be righted. In essence, this means you don't have to feel guilty, but you can ask yourself what you might be able to contribute to the healing process.

BECOMING VISIBLE

There is reason to hope that the invisible child, the one who appears lost to his brothers, can become visible. This may be the first step in the healing process among men of different cultures: "Let me see you, my brother, and help me to understand you that we might walk together." That is appropriate, for as the Lakota tribe declares, "Mitakue Oyasin": "We are all related" (see Ephesians 3:14–21).

TAKE ACTION

1. As a non-Indian, try to understand the Indian man's perspective by completing the following exercise. Imagine yourself as an Indian child separated from your parents, being told you are a coward, and being given a new name and clothing to wear. You have had your long hair cut and are being told that the white ways are good but Indian ways are bad. On a sheet of paper complete the following:

   a. As an Indian child, I feel _____

   _____.

   b. As an Indian child, I think (or feel) that my family _____

   _____.

   c. My thoughts about white people are _____

   _____.

2. As an American-Indian man, what response of acculturation do you have to white society—assimilation, rejection, biculturalism, or deculturation? Why? After reading this chapter, do you feel this is the best response?

3. As a non-Indian man, read 2 Samuel 21: What attitude did David exemplify? What was God's response when David made restitution? How do you feel about taking responsibility for the sins of your race? How can you "contribute to the healing process" (p. 95)?

4. The author holds up John Perkins as a model of forgiveness. As an Indian man, what was your reaction to the story? What holds you back from forgiveness?

CHAPTER SIX

The Hispanic Male: The Mascot

BY JESSE MIRANDA

Y ou may have met Hispanic men and women in the past couple years. In California one of every six people has a Spanish surname; in Los Angeles, one of every two has that surname. Demographers, those who study population trends and chart people's backgrounds, talk of the "browning of America." As those of Hispanic descent increase in numbers in major cities, demographers predict they will be the dominant minority in the twenty-first century in a nation that will be dominated by non-caucasian groups.

And whether you have talked with a Hispanic or not, you probably have your own image of the Hispanic male. How would you describe the Hispanic man in terms of his actions and attitudes?

Typically the Hispanic man plays the role of the mascot. We see him playing the role of comic relief and comforter within the family. In most cases he actually does play that role willingly, though his reasons and his heart are misunderstood. In many cases that role is forced on him. We will look at his family role shortly.

THE HISPANIC IDENTITY

Who is the Hispanic man? If you are a non-Hispanic reader, watch out for the stereotype that all Hispanics are alike. One biographer of the Hispanic experience asked Marguerite, a Latino woman, for advice she would give those who are trying to understand her people. "Just tell them who we are and that we are not all alike."[1]

Hers is good advice. Hispanic Americans are a diverse people who share a common heritage, and their fiercely guarded diversity is at once their glory and undoing. That diversity is also the cornerstone of their existence. Let's meet the Hispanic man.

From Twenty-six Countries

As we saw in a previous chapter, there is no one masculine template for all males to follow. This is especially true of the Hispano. There is no typical Hispanic male. Hispanos are not one nationality, one culture, but many. We are Mexican (61 percent), Puerto Rican (15 percent), Cuban (6 percent), and of Central and South American origins (10 percent), among others. We come from twenty-six nations.

Hispano or Latino?

For the purposes of this chapter, the gender term *Hispano* for the Hispanic male will be used to address two of the salient issues—identity and diversity—affecting the more than 25 million persons of Hispanic descent in this country. The names may be confusing, as Mexicans often prefer the designation *Chicanos*, and Puerto Ricans like to be called *Boricuas*. We, like other men, are after the quest for freedom and conquest of poverty—poverty of goods and of the soul.

The American Hispano usually will identify himself as either Hispano or Latino. Significantly, the deciding factor is where and how he thinks Hispanic history begins. He is influenced by who he thinks were the subjects—the ones who acted, the dignified ones—and who were the objects—the people whom the forces of history acted upon. The term *Latino* refers to the Indian or indigenous side of this history, which originated in this continent. *Hispano,* on the other hand, pertains to ancient Spain or European bloodline. In the Southwest United States, the term *Latino* is preferred, while in other regions, especially in New Mexico where I was born, *Hispano* is more readily used. Generally, the terms are interchangeable.

This chapter focuses on developing a better understanding of the Hispano. If you desire to minister effectively to your Hispanic brother, clearly you need a greater cultural and spiritual understanding of who he is. More than simply learning to better cope with cultural differences, you want to know the Hispano better in order to facilitate healthy cultural and spiritual interaction. The result will be greater cooperation, and we can build a better man, a better church, and a better society.

Kierkegaard's goal "To will to be himself is man's true vocation" is a good beginning. As a Hispano, I believe I am more myself to the degree that I am free to be able to participate with my neighbors and with Christ to create strategies for cooperation.

Yet like all other men, Hispanos feel the need to do well. Blocking the way to the progress of Hispanos have been several obstacles. It is essential that we point out some of the obstacles, most of which arise from misunderstandings of who the Hispano is. Three of these have been (and continue to be): (1) the false assumptions that Hispanos are a recent immigrant group to this country and not native to the Southwest as history testifies; (2) a hostile relationship between Hispanos and the dominant society, which began with the acquisition of contiguous territory and internal colonialism; and (3) the research that has reinforced a negative conception and profile of Hispanos. Those studies depict the Hispanic man as (a) controlled and manipulated by traditional culture, (b) docile, passive, present-oriented, fatalistic, and lacking in achievement, (c) coming from a family governed by an authoritarian system, dominated by the cult of machismo, and (d) violent and prone to antisocial and criminal behavior.

Those misunderstandings about the Hispano's identity have caused many non-Hispanics to think that most of the problems encountered by Hispanos are the result of deficiencies in their own culture and family system. Without developing relationships with Hispanos, we are left to think all Hispanos are docile or dominated by machismo. That isn't so. My friend Pablo remembers a wise father who spurred him to achieve. "Don't let anyone tell you you can only be a good automobile mechanic," his dad said. "You can be a math scientist if you apply yourself. It runs in your blood. Who do you think built pyramids in Mexico prior to the white man stepping on this continent?"

Another friend, Daniel, is an elementary school teacher in California who knows about the deception of believing in machismo. "In high school and in college sociology classes I read about the Hispanic male macho man, but at home and in my neighborhood I found loving, hardworking, and responsible fathers."

PLAYING THE MASCOT

At the beginning of the chapter we mentioned that the Hispano sometimes willingly plays the mascot. He provides comic relief, being fun-loving and caring. But he does it to seek attention. In truth, he feels more despair than happiness. If you have a Hispanic friend whose playful demeanor strikes you as "happy-go-lucky," be aware that his demeanor isn't so much rooted in the joy of the present as fear of the future.

One man told me once, "Canto y rio por no llorar" ("I sing and laugh so as not to cry"). Another admitted that "Otros toman para olvidarse, yo tomo para confessar" ("Some drink to forget himself, I drink to confess"). The cheerful demeanor of the Hispanic mascot is a cover-up; inside the pain is real, and he wants and appreciates other men who care and accept him as he is.

THE HISPANO'S ANXIETY

Like African-American, Native-American, and Asian-American men, the Hispanic man is under examination. While the African-American male is judged by the color of his skin, the Hispano is judged by his usefulness. Neither feels his worth under such examination. Like other men of color, Hispanos suffer from performance anxiety. And we have the same emotions: we feel alienated, powerless, and angry, though perhaps for different reasons.

Unlike others, the root of the Hispano's anxiety lies in the unique and recurring patterns of his (1) mestizo history (mixed blood—Indian, black, Spanish), (2) colonialized culture, and (3) ostracized religion—the Roman Catholic church, whose power was similar to that of a state within a state—that weighs heavily on his performance in his family and in his society.

These orientations form his identity, explain his diversity, and shape his worldview. They are the reason for the anger and fear the Hispano feels as he struggles to be himself and as he faces the challenges of the future. "We are neither Europeans nor Indians," said Simon Bolivar, "but an intermediate species between the aboriginal and the Spanish. Americans by birth, Europeans by birth . . . so our case is most extraordinary and complicated."[2]

Only by appreciating how these elements operate in the Hispano's background can you understand the Hispano's behavior and then begin to build a positive relationship with him.

Mixed Parentage

Ultimately, the distinctiveness that counts lies in each man's version of himself. It is most difficult for a person of mixed ancestry, as in the case of the Hispano, to choose any one version. I am not sure that the Hispanic man really knows himself. The fact is that three distinct strands have converged to provide the Hispano's cultural heritage to some degree or another—the Spanish, the Amerindian, and the African.

A man who is mestizo (mixed parentage) has a shifting place of origin. He is Hispano one day and Latino the next. That is, one day he looks toward his European bloodline and on another day toward his Latin American origins. He exhibits the dualistic spirit in the Latino personality. He is the dreamer or the realist. One day he may be the conquistador and the next he may be the conquered one. He has inherited the contrasting, and, yes, often contradictory tendencies and values that are evident in Hispanos in the U.S. In Latin America he may be the crusader of freedom or the ruthless dictator that stamps out all vestiges of freedom. In the U.S. he may see himself as the guest or as the dispossessed. But always he is condemned by the complexity of his nature to an endless examination of his own blood. This is his greatest dilemma.

The history of the Hispano, says Shorris,[3] is a confused and painful addition of race plus culture plus conquest. It has been a bitter and bloody history. Manny Ortiz, in his book *The Hispanic Challenge,* reminds us that "we must keep in mind that Hispanics first came to this country not through migration but rather through expansion, purchase or military overthrow. Without question annexation has figured into this process."[4]

This process is responsible for what many see as the polychromatic character and behavioral schizophrenic life of the Hispano. He is the Mascot, happy yet, in truth, sad. Historical destiny placed Hispanic men in the midst of two worlds which were only partially theirs. They are no longer European, because they live in America; nor are they Americans, because their inherent nature preserves their European sense of life. This initial psychological conflict has affected the particular events of our history.

The Colonized Culture

The Hispano looks at his mixed ancestry and is reminded of his history. The conquerors destroyed the surviving adult males and bred with the women, creating a new race of mixed bloods. The crushing conquests stripped the Hispano of his dignity. Those first Spaniard conquistadors came motivated by gold, glory, and (so they said) God, but the brutal conquests, which included marrying their subjects, stripped the Hispano of his dignity. The annexation and expansionist treaties that followed linked conquest and imperialistic purposes in the mind of the Hispano. Mexican-Americans are probably the most angry among Hispanos. They remind us that they never came to the U.S.; rather the U.S. came to them in another display of annexation. More than money or position, the Hispano feels stripped of his honor, or *de su honor.*

The Hispano carries in him the typical personality traits of oppressed people who have internalized the images and notions of an oppressor. He believes he has been denied full disclosure of his history and has been cut off from his own culture and heritage. He also largely regards religion as an emblem, a justification and an excuse for greed. The end result is a Mascot in disguise, someone whose mask serves to cover some deep-seated feelings. His surface laughter is indeed shallow.

Samuel Ramos, professor of philosophy at the University of Mexico, characterizes a Hispanic personality in terms of certain basic psychological notions—distrust, resulting in a sense of inferiority and pessimism; resentment of criticism, with marked tendency to react defensively and to quarrel; and passionate aggression. He too has learned the common rules of other men of color: (1) Do not trust, (2) Do not feel, (3) Do not talk. These are the dangerous effects of a history of colonialism and annexation on the character of the Hispano.[5]

LA RAZA AND EL PUEBLO—ETHNICITY

"There are times in the history of persons and people, particularly times of crisis . . . when the awakening of a sense of heritage becomes a potent determinant of destiny,"[6] writes Eldin Villafane. If history is considered the reason and cause of the Hispano's diversity, then culture is the anchor of his identity. History still governs his mind/thought. Culture exists to provide some identity. Pluralism becomes his way of life. This is the history and culture of Hispanos in the United States, who differ in so many ways: their duration in the U.S., their subgroups or nationalities, and their character from subgroup to subgroup (Mexican, Puerto Rican, Cuban, Central and South American).

Despite those differences, the Hispano's culture has many similarities from subgroup to subgroup. History has left him with many customs and a common language. More importantly, a shared feeling of "peoplehood" (race and ethnicity) has emerged in Hispanics under the names of *la raza* and *el pueblo*. These terms, according to Villafane,

> have become rich cultural and political symbols of togetherness, community, and way of life—integrating language, family custom, tradi-

tions, and other spiritual and cultural traits. The word "raza" can be narrowly translated as "the race," but its implications are far more complex. "Pueblo" refers to both the town and the people living in it.[7]

When you are ready to develop a relationship with a Hispanic man, don't be surprised at his desire to maintain closer ties with his own race. The power of *la raza* creates an intimacy you cannot duplicate. And that is OK. As Rudy Gonzales wrote in *Prophets Denied Honor,* "I have come a long way to nowhere, unwillingly dragged by that monstrous, technical industrial giant—called progress and Anglo success. . . . I look at myself. I watch my brothers. I shed tears of sorrow. I sow seeds of hate. I withdraw to the safety within the circle of life . . . *mi raza* (my own people)."[8]

KEY HISPANIC VALUES

What are the values and cultural traits of a Hispanic man? Villafane provides us with the portrait of the Hispano who has endured the crisis over many generations. The Hispano, who Villafane terms "Homos Hispanicus," displays eight distinctive traits, ranging from "personalismo"—making personal relations paramount, above abstract principles and institutions—to "romerias"—a sense of timeliness to be cultivated. Other traits of "Homos Hispanicus" are:

Passion. Life is to be heroic. Feelings/emotions are to be accepted in a wholistic response to life.

The paradox of the soul. The Hispano is both a realist and idealist. One can be both without confusion or confinement.

Community. Communal consciousness permeates all of life.

Musical elan. He expresses unity, liberation, transcendence, and joy in all of life.

"Fiesta." He engages in celebration, affirming that life is a gift and worth living.

Family. The Hispanic man accepts intimate group relations for a sense of security, identity, and recognition of accomplishments. At the same time, he accepts that ambiguous cultural trait known as "machismo."[9]

We will examine the final value, the family, to better understand how the Hispano will value friendships outside the family as well as relationships within.

La Familia

Hispanos think and act as a family unit. The family is the main unit in the Hispano's community, superseding church, political parties, or any other group. On any spring or summer weekend, you're likely to find dozens of Hispanic families at their local park, playing games, listening to festive music, and enjoying barbecues. If the son or dad (often both) is in a soccer league, most of the family will show up and cheer him on. Family solidarity and a collective sense of personhood prevails in the Hispano culture.

This emphasis on family identity runs contrary to Western individualism and its increased autonomy. This value is so deep in the Hispanic culture that a Hispanic child is taught to take care of his brothers and sisters even to the point of missing school. Many non-Hispanics do not recognize or else do not respect such values, as they seek to unwittingly impose or else inculcate values alien to another's community. For instance, the child who stays home to help care for a sick brother or sister typically will be punished by a school system that values attendance except for personal illness. The child is confused by two conflicting messages/values.

With the Hispano's high regard for families, familial esteem has historically been more crucial than self-esteem. A Hispanic man will find his primary identity more in kinship (ethnicity) and filial piety than in individual self-actualization. As Villafane notes, "The values of family well-being overrides in importance individual well-being."[10] Thus his relationships are intimate, personal, and basic.

Jose told me about his white friends asking him one day, "Can you say how being Hispanic affects your life?" Jose wasn't sure how to reply, but his eventual answer indicates the family identity that most Hispanics feel.

"Well, I don't know how it affects me," Jose first answered. "It's just there; you know, like something that was there before I was born, and it'll be there after I'm gone."

"But what does being Hispanic mean to you?" one of his friends persisted.

"You mean besides beans and tortillas?" Jose answered, laughing aloud. Then turning serious, he added, "I'm not sure exactly how to answer that. It means family, I guess. That's the big thing with Hispanics—family. You go to see relatives on weekends, on vacations—you meet more cousins and uncles than you knew you had." The Hispano thinks of his worth and identity in terms of his family membership and relationship.

El Machismo

The issue of machismo stirs controversy and confusion. Machismo expresses itself in a variety of ways; yet any analysis of this trait must begin with a study of the family, for it is here that the tensions are the most severe. It is in the context of the family that this theme develops many implications for the rest of the Hispano life.

We can define machismo as "authority and strong leadership manifested by the Hispanic man." Nathan Murillo states that machismo is "an important part of using authority within the family in a just and fair manner." Some see in "machismo" a desirable combination of virtues of courage and fearlessness in man—the head and protector of the family, responsible for its well-being.

On the other hand, this Latin ideal of masculine valor has been closely identified with being strongly masculine in sexual capacity and general behavior since medieval times. The invading conquistadors exerted dominance over native women. They considered themselves *muy macho* as they came to the new world without their families to exploit and then return to Europe. Machismo dates back to the Muslim society, a culture which deeply and directly influenced Spanish culture for six hundred years. The orthodox experience of Islam may well have helped to develop or reinforce Spanish devotion to masculine heroism, patriarchalism, patron-client dependencies, and the repression of the feminine.

Since that time it is a form of male chauvinism that has become a questionable trait of Hispano culture here and abroad. Machismo is simply male dominance. Being constantly motivated to exhibit his dominance also produces a measure of insecurity in the female. Machismo, of course, depends on the woman's cooperation. To Hispanos, a real man is one who has his wife and children in complete subjection. The Hispanic man's insecurity best illustrates machismo by his constant fear of betrayal by women and by his need for power and dominance.

WHAT HISPANICS CAN DO

This discussion has acknowledged the misunderstandings, insensitivity, and even abuse that Hispanics have experienced. For reconciliation to occur and friendships to develop, non-Hispanics must do their part. (See next section, "What Non-Hispanics Can Do.") However, reconciliation also requires action by my Hispanic brothers. Here are three things Hispanos can do to promote friendships with other races.

1. Know and Speak the English Language

Many Hispanos still tend to believe that the primary determining fact of true Hispanic identity is language, and in the Hispanic communities of America there are vast bilingual populations.[11] In 1988, only 10 percent of the Hispano population used English exclusively.

Someone once said, "Language is the house of being and the residence of humanity." Hispanics need not surrender their language, yet a strong reliance on Spanish within the community raises an important issue, according to Ortiz: "whether we are thinking in North American ideologies."[12] This is true particularly if Hispanos desire to help shape these ideologies—ideologies based on understanding, love, and justice.

Many Hispanos keep their language as a matter of pride and identity. This is to be respected, but an important question must be asked, Does it communicate? Language is a serious issue in Hispanic communities, families, and churches, a matter of communication between generations and social and economic differences. Our purpose for the use of a language is not simply to help us better cope with cultural differences between us and others but to facilitate cultural synergy or cooperative results through this medium for all peoples.

A problem occurs when Spanish is the "private language" at home and English is the "public language" of the marketplace or society, creating a gap between values learned at home and values of the society. Just as family is the basic unit of the social system, so language is the basic unit of the system of thought. Through language we think, understand, remember, and communicate with others. We must be able to speak the majority language of English.

2. Respect the Values of the Prevailing Culture

While we Hispanos must hold to the uniqueness of our own values, basing our identity on the values representative of our struggle as Hispanic people, we must be fully aware that others hold different values and assumptions. Those values are legitimate even when they are directly opposite to our own. We must respect them and the people who hold them, even as we would want non-Hispanics to respect our values.

3. Forgive Past Injustices and Find a New Meaning

As Hispanos we must forgive the injustices of the past and move on to a new existence. An Angolan proverb says, "The person who throws stones forgets; the one who is hit never forgets." We cannot forget our past—that is our history, our roots. But we cannot constantly try to explain a deep personal experience to someone who has never had a similar experience. Instead, let us move on to a new meaning and a new experience.

I have noted that the Mexican-American often feels anger over the conquests of parts of his former land. Many Spanish feel anger as well. After wars and treaties, the Spanish seemingly gave up their claims, principally along the southern borders of the U.S. But the descendants have not forgotten. Hispanics of the third and fourth generations are known for focusing on the injustices of the past. A college student confessed, saying, "We are like the Jews. We do not want the world to forget what we have suffered. We remember the conquests (by Spain and the Manifest Destiny) and the injuries, review the violations, and ruminate on the hurts. For the most part, we view the white population's westward expansion as an act of aggression against the native peoples."

Many Hispanos feel that injustices continue, with discrimination in employment and housing at the forefront of a list of injustices. Yet we Hispanos cannot hold in anger without becoming bitter or blocking the development of friendships. As Jeff King noted in his call to Native-Americans, we too must begin the move to reconciliation by forgiving our white brothers and seeking the restoration of love to which Christ has called us.

There is a Spanish saying, "Between the hammer and a pliers do not stick your nose." To reach out to other cultures is not "sticking one's nose" in other people's business. It is, in fact, kingdom business. No matter what definitions of who we are emerge from the sociologists, in our inner being we know that we are *un pueblo naciendo . . . un pueblo marchado hacia el futuro que ya ha comendzado* ("A people marching toward the future that has already begun.") We have within us (and to some extent within our context) some control; more importantly our opportunities come from the Lord.

HOW NON-HISPANICS CAN HELP

Here are some tips that anyone may employ to reach out to Hispanic men:

1. Be Bible-centered

Scripture affirms and transcends culture. All people are His creation. His church is made of people from "every tribe, every tongue, and every nation." His orders are cross-cultural, "to all the world."

Therefore, embrace the biblical mandate to love one another, including your Hispanic brothers.

Furthermore, Jesus has made it clear that believers are to demonstrate their oneness with each other. In this way, we show a doubting world the truth of the gospel. As He told His disciples, such unity with our brothers lets "the world know that you sent me and have loved them even as you have loved me" (John 17:23).

2. Be Culturally Prepared

Forewarned is forearmed. This chapter has been an introduction to many of the distinctives of Hispanic culture. Consider additional reading and individual or group study and training to understand cultural factors in general or specifics. As you meet with Hispanos, admit your ignorance and ask them to talk about their culture, and then show respect for their values and opinions. One Mexican immigrant observed how little we know about his people and said, "Americans know more about their enemies than about their friends."

Analyze the other culture as to: (1) communication style, (2) time sense, (3) values and business ethics, (4) work habits and practices, and (5) family and marriage. Learn about their customs, traditions, and beliefs. For instance, unlike Anglos who typically identify themselves by what they "do," Hispanos usually identify themselves by who they are. Thus an Anglo-American will identify himself by saying, "I am a teacher" or "I am a plumber;" the Hispanic-American will say, "I am the son of . . ." or "I come from . . . " Similarly, Anglos are pragmatic and like to "get to the point" during a conversation, while Hispanics are philosophical and usually indirect in their comments. Non-Hispanics sometimes mistakenly call this "beating around the bush."

3. Be Culturally Sensitive

Avoid criticizing other practices and procedures while using the standard of one's culture for comparison purposes. Being aware of another's culture will make one more acceptable.

Recognize as a follower of God that the gospel and every person on earth are fathered by the same God. For a greater sensitivity to the cultures around you, including the Hispanic culture, reread the Gospels with a cultural perspective, focusing on how Jesus acknowledged the cultural elements of the day (such as the Samaritan woman in John 4), including the differing cultural beliefs. Then consider how the dynamics of contemporary American culture may modify the way you convey the gospel to a different culture. Though the gospel components will remain unchanged, the way you express the message will reflect the needs and emphases of the culture.

4. Avoid Stereotyping the Hispano

Remember that every Hispanic man is a distinct person; avoid stereotyping the Hispano according to his particular historical background. For example, not all Mexican men try to dominate women; neither are all Mexicans happy and docile. Not all Puerto Ricans are aggressive and feisty; neither are all Cubans daring. Recall Marguerite's advice in the beginning of this chapter: "Just tell them who we are and that we are not all alike." Hispanics are proud of the richness of the diversity within their culture.

5. Seek Personal Reconciliation with Hispanic Men

Reconciliation with Hispanic men must begin on the personal level, your time being devoted to impact at least one Hispanic by developing a personal relationship. I am not advocating that non-Hispanics try to undo, from top to bottom, the unjust structures that have caused injury to Hispanos. Nor am I advocating you enter a relationship in which you exchange with a Hispanic friend the superior and inferior roles of white and Hispanic communities. Instead, a personal relationship will mean both he and you work to (1) release the past with its pain, (2) restructure the present with new reciprocal respect and acceptance, and (3) look to the future by taking new risks and being spontaneous in the relationship.

A strong relationship between a Hispanic and non-Hispanic will be personal and express a mutual love in ways that are appropriate to the culture. When we do this, we will rid ourselves of the "us versus them" mentality.

TAKE ACTION

1. If you are a Hispanic reader, what behaviors of yours might be described as fun-loving or happy-go-lucky? Do these behaviors mask less happy emotions?

2. Page 99 lists some "traits" of Hispanos (including being docile, passive, and lacking in achievement). As a Hispano, do you view yourself this way? What about your brothers? As a non-Hispano man, how have these stereotypes kept you from developing relationships with Hispano men?

3. How does the language problem—"Should I speak English or is Spanish alone OK?"—contribute to the seeming schizophrenia of the Hispanic culture? As a non-Hispano, do you view language as society's problem or a problem of Hispanos only?

CHAPTER SEVEN

White Men Can't Jump

BY E. GLENN WAGNER

I n high school I used to go to an inner-city YMCA to play "city ball."
That's slammin', jammin', no-blood, no-foul, and no-wimps-allowed
basketball. It's a brutal sport, but great fun. I'm a white guy and a
lot of the other teens were black. Every time I showed up at the "Y," my
black friends would fill the air with fun-loving insults about the other
players' abilities, the so-called "trash talk." When it came to trash talking with the white guy, racist talk was included. "White men can't
jump," they said (and a whole lot more!). Long before they made a
movie featuring that stereotype, I heard it on the "Y" basketball court.

Cultural stereotypes either leave you bitter or leave you better.
Being told what you "can't do" because of your racial or ethnic group
identification can move you to excel beyond your peers and your critics, or those stereotypes can become demoralizing, self-fulfilling
prophecies. At the "Y," I tried to prove them wrong—that white men
can jump. Yet I also wanted desperately to be accepted just for who I
was—even if I couldn't out-jump all my inner-city friends. My strategy
worked.

STEREOTYPES FOR WHITES

But while facing one cultural stereotype head-on and winning
friends on the basketball court, I was facing another demoralizing
stereotype in school. This one I succumbed to.

On the first day of my sophomore year in high school, I was
ushered in to see the guidance counselor, who was also our school's

football coach. This unexpected appointment had me feeling curious and very anxious. Upon arriving at his office and taking a seat, I watched as he dramatized my fate. He pulled out a manila folder from his filing cabinet, opened it, shuffled the stack of papers, spread them on his desk, put his hand on them, and then made this chilling pronouncement: "Glenn, what's in this folder tells me you don't have what it takes to go to college. I suggest you learn a trade so that you will be able to make your way in this world."

I was quickly enrolled in a vocational/technical school, handed a piece of paper for my parents to sign, and encouraged to let them know that this move was best for me. Our meeting was over in all of ten minutes.

Whereas I had never set any academic records up to this point, I was devastated to hear a man I respected tell me I was not bright enough to pursue what was touted as a "real career." Ironically, he underestimated the power of the vocational/technical school, because most of those men I went to that school with are doing quite well today—many owning their own businesses.

Stereotypes are powerful weapons. They bind us to our past, making it difficult to achieve today. They make us question ourselves. We can succeed but we must dismiss these false labels to do so. And we must dismiss those stereotypes we have of men from other cultures. This is crucial to finding reconciliation, man to man, in America.

Living under that negative stereotype that a "real" man went to a college (instead of a vocational school) placed upon me a heavy burden. When I finally graduated from high school, I tried a nearby junior college and didn't make it halfway through the first semester. I seemed bent on becoming what others told me I already was—a failure, someone who could never achieve or amount to much. I learned firsthand the sting and pain of having someone force their opinion on me and see it become a self-fulfilling prophecy.

Following my interrupted stint at college, I worked in a nearby factory. In my thirty-five-man work crew, I was the only white man. The first several weeks were extremely difficult. Through much tension and after much fighting, I was seeking to make a way for myself and to be accepted. Finally, Randy, a black man about thirty, took me under his wing. We became best of friends—I stayed at his house, ate with him, played with his children, and worked with him side by side. In both dangerous situations and fun times, we grew together.

When Randy introduced me to his larger circle of friends, I came to appreciate the great pain and difficulty these black men faced because of stereotypes foisted on them. We sat for hours talking about issues between whites and blacks and the injustices within our society. I struggled with their anger, their rhetoric, their strong positions. Because I was white, I was perceived as the one oppressing them and holding them down. It was as if I exercised all the power, while they had none.

IS IT A SIN TO BE WHITE?

That seemed like a stereotype too—that I was blamed for trying to hold them down. I was blamed for the injustice they experienced. I felt, at times, like I was put upon to solve their problems, to fix the political system that dealt so harshly with many minorities, to correct the economic disparities, and to help remove the barriers for advancement and employment. I was challenged time and time again with the statement "Whites simply don't care."

It didn't seem to matter that my mom had grown up in the inner city and was persecuted as a "minority" (my grandfather was an immigrant from Italy). It didn't matter that she had lived in poverty and had been forced to move eighteen times in the first ten years of her life—all because Grandpa had no job and no money to pay the rent. Was it a sin for me to be born white (as if I had some choice in the matter)?

Recently, in response to this question during a discussion at work on racial issues, a fellow staff member who is also an African-American told me, "An M & M® [candy] doesn't choose what color it's going to be." Simple words but true. His statement encouraged me and relieved much of my guilt and shame—feelings I had simply because I was white.

Many other whites are in need of that same release. Recently a black columnist and controversial talk-show host in Denver, Ken Hamblin, capitalized on this idea. Realizing it was time blacks let whites off the hook, Hamblin issued upon request thousands of "Certificates of Absolution." Why? To "free the Anglo millions" from white guilt, he explained.

Hamblin tapped into a real part of whites' uneasiness. We sometimes do feel guilty for the injustices to minority brothers, including blacks, and don't know what to do. What can we do? As I noted, racial stereotypes are difficult to get out from. Whether at play (on the basketball court) or work (at the factory), we can be stereotyped as those who don't care about the plight of our brothers of color. I was stereotyped as a white man who intentionally used power to hold them down. I was also stuck with the collective-guilt stigma: Every negative experience within the minority community is a direct result of my sin.

MEET THE ENABLER

Though it is difficult to outlive or undo such stereotypes and stigmas, we do have a choice to make as white Christian males. We can choose to continue to be either an enabler, one who succumbs to guilt and victimization, or an empowerer, one who builds relationships that facilitate men of color breaking out from their stereotypes, just as I need to break out from mine, to become all that God wants us to be.

Most of us white men play the role of enabler. This is the person in the family who provides and makes choices to compensate for those who feel powerless and dependent. This person often does not see the illness or the problems in the family, and when he does he feels guilty and tries to compensate by taking care of the person who is dependent or has the problem. As white enablers, we try to pretend the problem of discrimination against our minority brothers is minimal, and we try to compensate by helping blacks, Asians, Hispanics, and American Indians instead of empowering them.

BURDEN OR BENEFIT?

What can we do in the midst of the stereotypes? Which direction do I turn? You and I as white men are faced with several options.

The Detached Option

We could take on the out-of-sight, out-of-mind viewpoint. We could be detached and withdrawn, leaving race issues as a problem for others. *After all,* I thought, *my ancestors never owned slaves, nor did they ever hire migrant workers. So it's not my responsibility.* Maybe that's your thinking too.

The Political Option

As a second option, as white men we could consider the problem as purely an economic and political one. "Leave the race issues to politicians and to the wealthy. They can develop further entitlement programs and fund them to correct the problem," we may say. "I don't have a lot of money and I do not hold political office, so I'm really not able to help." Unless we are in government office or have money to give, there is nothing we can do to help—or so we think. As enablers, we often choose this option, thinking that with programs or money we can compensate and "take care" of the minority person. This often makes our minority brothers feel or act dependent on others.

The Rescue Option

A third option is to take on racial reconciliation as a "white man's burden," believing that as white men we are the savior of the races. But if I take that posture, I'll treat those of other races not as equals but as children to be patronized, disciplined, and taught. Rather than developing a peer relationship, I'd be entering into a parent-child relationship. The enabler also contributes to this patronizing and dependent attitude.

The Guilt Option

A fourth response is to simply let guilt overwhelm us. That is how some whites felt while viewing and reliving the events portrayed in the movie *Mississippi Burning,* which showed whites lynching blacks. But its effect on some white viewers was like one powerful image in that film: a noose seemed to tighten around the white man's neck. Whenever you felt the injustice and saw the white perpetrator, guilt yanked upon the rope, and you felt the lynching was your own.

Guilt actually makes it possible for the one in the role of victim to control the other. For instance, in an alcoholic/abusive home, very often the sober, responsible spouse is made to feel shame and shoulder blame. That spouse either does that which she knows is wrong (enabling, or covering up for the alcoholic or abuser), or she ends up not following through with what she knows is right. Such an abused spouse has come to believe that the beatings are her fault. In *Mississippi Burning,* it was the beaten-down sheriff's wife who eventually turned in her husband and stemmed the tide of racism in that town.

Biblical conviction differs from guilt feelings. Biblical conviction—often brought on by a combination of circumstances, the Holy Spirit, the Bible, and sound preaching—leads to confession, repentance, and empowerment by God. By His all-sufficient grace we are set on a positive course of action. But guilt—often brought on by circumstances that are misinterpreted and emotions that are manipulated—brings frustration, bitterness, and powerlessness. By distorted human reasoning, we come to feel helpless and despair of hope.

The Biblical Option

The final option is the best—and it is the most biblical. As white men who are the majority in the American culture, we choose to re-

115

gard racial reconciliation as a God-given mandate and opportunity. This is the biblical option. The biblical mandate is clear, with several implications.

Here are four beliefs we must accept for reconciliation to take place, to enact that biblical option. The beliefs are necessary if we are to fulfill God's mandate to come together, brother to brother.

BELIEFS NEEDED FOR RECONCILIATION

Admit to the Racism

We whites first must be willing to acknowledge that racism exists in various forms—both subtle and blatant, individual and institutional. Often outside programs and activities, in such places as schools, churches, and the workplace, contribute to attitudes and behaviors that convey whites are superior to nonwhite racial groups. Eventually this influences our personal beliefs. Our beliefs of another person's inferiority can be as subtle as a racist viewpoint concerning work ethic and laziness or as blatant as refusing service to black patrons of your restaurant.

We must recognize that racism has been institutionalized in various government regulations, political policies, and social customs. When laws are passed in Congress with the sole purpose of maintaining the socioeconomic advantages of whites over nonwhites, this is institutional racism. In more subtle forms, we see this in the local country club, in the sheriff's arrest records, and in our bank's lending policies to potential homeowners and businessmen. Its most blatant and cruel form has appeared as near genocide or a rigid caste system, as happened in the Nazism of Germany and the apartheid of South Africa.

Racism also exists in a cultural form. We see this every time the products of the white majority culture—language, traditions, appearance, music, mores, and values—are held up as the norm, or even as superior to the values of nonwhite culture.

To one degree or another, from one family to the next, and from one generation to the next, racism does exist and is perpetuated within all of us. For lasting racial reconciliation to take place, racist views must be abandoned and a biblical outlook and belief system established. This leads to the second plank in any racial reconciliation platform.

Believe that God Has Created Every Man As an Equal

Second, we must understand that all people have been created in the image of God (Genesis 1:27). As such, there is no greater nor lesser amount of God's image in any one human being or ethnic group. This foundational truth undercuts any attempt at superiority. An argument about which race is superior cannot be supported from Scripture and only leads to further division.

We must know and believe what the Scriptures say about God's creation and valuing of each of us, no matter our color or background. The Scriptures disavow the claims of any one people to be superior. Those within God's forever community of faith may be chosen, but they are not choice.

> Brothers, think of what you were when you were called. Not many of you were wise by human standards; not many were influential; not many were of noble birth. But God chose the foolish things of the world to shame the wise; God chose the weak things of the world to shame the strong. He chose the lowly things of this world and the despised things—and the things that are not—to nullify the things that are, so that no one may boast before him. (1 Corinthians 1:26–29)

While I am all for pride in one's heritage and ethnic background, such cultural pride frequently has deteriorated to the point that people will feel better about themselves only if they can be convinced that they are superior to other people. The rhetoric about racial pride often emphasizes the superiority claims and racial put-downs, not the legitimate self-affirming pride in one's heritage.

Recognize the Oneness of People in Christ

If you are a Christian, delivered from the penalty of your sins by Jesus Christ, recognize a key point in racial reconciliation is accepting what the Bible says about *all* believers, whatever race or nation: we all (slave and free) are part of one body in Jesus Christ (1 Corinthians 12:13; Galatians 3:28). As the apostle Paul wrote, if one member of the body hurts, we all hurt together (1 Corinthians 12:26). When other men—not only white men but brown, yellow, black, and red men—are in pain, feeling disconnected from the body of Christ, I have a biblical responsibility to minister to them.

Generally, we are to minister to others as we would have them do unto us (Luke 6:31). That means honoring one another above ourselves (Romans 12:10), bearing one another's burden (Galatians 6:2), and forgiving each other (Ephesians 4:32). We are to serve one another, love one another, and look out for the best interests of the other—all because we belong to Christ (Philippians 2:3–4). Thus, I develop relationships, affirming the value of those parts that suffer the most. One brother might be a hand and another a foot, but both are essential to the smooth functioning of the body. But these first three demonstrations of racial reconciliation require a fourth ingredient.

Speak and Act with Humility

Fourth, if we are to do our best to "live in harmony with one another" (1 Peter 3:8), we will "be willing to associate with people of low position" and "not be conceited" (Romans 12:16). For this we need humility. Humility is a necessary ingredient to living at peace with all the different ethnic groups that make up the body of Christ (Ephesians 4:2–3). We are to act justly and preach grace, which is impossible unless it springs from a humble heart (Hosea 6:8).

If we acknowledge all forms of racism within our midst, if we affirm the variety and equality of all people created by God, and if we rightly view the body of Christ as interdependent and united by the Spirit in the bond of peace, then in humility we will preach the grace of God and act justly in the midst of injustice. The practical implications of this four-plank platform are staggering:

- It means I will commit myself to building relationships that facilitate another, as well as myself, to become the man that God has called me to be.

- It means I will judge a man by the content of his character, not by the color of his skin.

- It means I will exercise my citizen's right to vote in a just manner, voting with a biblically informed conscience.

- It means my main responsibility will be to live out relationships and seek opportunities that reconcile men to God and men to one another.

WHAT WHITES CAN DO

Several steps can help you begin the process of reconciliation and connecting with men of other ethnic backgrounds. If you are a white American, here are five steps you can take.

1. Be Willing to Pay the Price

Baby steps are necessary when you begin something new. In trying to develop relationships with men of another race, you will at times attempt to engage a man in conversation, trying to be understanding, and then find that he will "get in your face." The anger, hurt, pain, and resentment built up over the years will come pouring out.

If you are not prepared for that, you will become defensive and simply write him off as another "angry black man" and have nothing more to do with him. So carefully consider whether you are willing to pay the price to be obedient to God in this area.

2. Perseverance is Necessary

After you pay the initial price, be willing to stick with it. Relationships take time to build and develop, because every relationship comes to a point where it can go either way. Whether coaching a Little League baseball team among inner city youth or tutoring them in computer skills, there will come a time when your key player or student doesn't show or follow through on a promise. Then you will be tempted to call for higher commitment or call it quits. When that inevitable conflict hits the fan, perseverance will enable you to work it through and be the stronger for it.

3. Appreciate His Pain

In the midst of this relationship-building, you can readily rationalize away the plight or minimize the pain of a persecuted minority. If you are tempted to discount what a victim of discrimination is feeling, I remind you that facts, perceptions, and feelings do not always agree. (Remember Rod's story of the carp who did not go for his food, even after the glass partition in the aquarium was removed?)

We can argue from the basis of facts and show what economic opportunities are available; however, the issue is not the facts but the perceptions and feelings that lie behind them. Allow your new friend to express his feelings, then give legitimacy to those feelings.

4. Make a Commitment to Reconciliation, One Relationship at a Time

If you are married, I encourage you and your family as a whole to make a commitment to build relationships of honor, to build relationships that empower, to build relationships that encourage each individual to change and become more of the kind of person God wants him to be. If you are an equal opportunity employer, this may lead you to give on-the-job training and mentoring to an unemployed or disadvantaged minority person whose character qualities warrant the extra investment of time and energy.

5. Make a Commitment That Looks Toward Future Generations

If you are a parent and want to share your home and heart with another, this may lead you into a foster-care program. Giving a home to children left abandoned in crack houses or neglected on the streets of despair could also lead you into mentoring relationships with the birth mother and adoptive parents. If you are choosing role models for your own children, consider cross-cultural friendships that could develop from your participation in racially mixed neighborhood get-togethers, school programs, summer camps, alternative worship experiences, and cultural exchange programs.

WHAT MEN OF COLOR CAN DO

Several steps can help minority men begin the process of reconciliation and to connect with white men. In Scripture, both the one who has done the offending and the offended are commanded to seek forgiveness and to reconcile a relationship. So instead of waiting for someone else, here's a brief game plan.

1. Release the White Man from Guilt

Be cautious and sincere in how you approach the white man. Communicate honestly the depth of the pain and even anger you are feeling, but do so in a nonmanipulative way. Allow the Spirit of God to use your words and those of the Scriptures to produce a God-wrought conviction that will lead to positive action.

2. Appreciate His Confusion

Many white men are confused and frustrated, which often comes from feeling powerless. The caucasian has probably heard much talk about the problem but little talk about significant ways to make a difference. What may seem to be indifference at times may be confusion as to what he should or should not do, paralyzing him into inaction.

3. Invite the White Man into Your World

Start to invite whites to various holiday gatherings that celebrate your cultural heritage, such as a Cinco de Mayo party or a Martin Luther King, Jr., observance. A church that I pastored had several language congregations that were a part of our fellowship. One of the highlights of the year for my family and me was being invited to attend the Chinese New Year celebration. Cultural walls were broken down, and an increased love and respect for another's culture were matured.

When whites mingle with you and your culture on your turf, several things happen. They see you relaxed, as you are with friends and family during celebration; this will help in developing a friendship. They also understand your heritage better, as they learn historical and cultural truths about the identity and value of your people and yourself. Finally, they begin to question their stereotypes about your culture, as they mingle with others of your culture in a relaxed setting that highlights their joy and strengths as a people.

4. Be Willing to Pay the Price

As we noted in our first two suggestions to the white reader, it will take time to forge life-transforming, and eventually community-transforming, relationships. Time, time, and more time are the main ingredients to developing a successful relationship. But it's worth it. Stick with it and watch God work.

As you respond with honor, so God will honor your efforts. What goes around comes around.

TAKE ACTION

1. As a white man, what stereotypes have you faced? Have you faced instances of anger or blame? How did you respond? What other ways could you have responded? The author talked about self-fulfilling prophecies in his own life (p. 112). As a nonwhite man, what is your attitude toward stereotypes of whites?

2. Discuss the difference between racial pride and racial superiority. How can you practice racial pride while letting others celebrate theirs? Read 1 Corinthians 12:13, 26; Galatians 3:28; 6:2; Romans 12:10; Ephesians 4:32; Philippians 2:3–4. How do these verses relate to your relationships with other men?

3. For both whites and non-whites, two common elements in developing friendships are paying the price and persevering. Set a goal this month of beginning or deepening a relationship with a man of another culture.

CHAPTER EIGHT
Who Am I? Who Are You?

In 1991 I had an exciting and scary experience while attending my twenty-year high school reunion. I must admit that I was more than curious to see what changes had taken place in my classmates. I wanted to see if the person voted "most likely to succeed" had and if the prom queen still had her youthful good looks.

When I entered the gym where the reunion was being held, I immediately recognized several people. They had put on a few pounds and grayed a little, but overall they looked the same. For others, though, I had to take out my yearbook and make a wild guess as to who they were. I feared if they greeted me by name I would be embarrassed that I wouldn't be able to do the same.

The conversations mostly centered around jobs, children, and retirement. These topics were a far cry from where we were twenty years ago. Some had gotten divorced and were on their second go-round, and others had married their high school sweethearts. But I did notice one major change—our perspective on life. The past twenty years of living had given all of us a different view of life.

Now instead of worrying about how we looked, we worried about what we had and where we would end up. Instead of focusing on how much we had lost, we now were focusing on how much we had left.

The next day I preached in the church where I had grown up. The pastor who knew me when I was first called into the ministry said, "Son, you sure have changed in your preaching. Before, you had to say something. Now, you have something to say."

Life has a way of changing your perspective and helps you to mature. In fact, even our Lord went through a growth process. Luke 2:52 says that "Jesus increased in wisdom and stature; in favor with God and with man." Jesus developed intellectually, physically, spiritually, and socially.

Where you are in your own growth process affects your perspective and has a lot to do with how you will live from day to day; it also will affect the types of relationships we have in life. When it comes to racial reconciliation and relationships, our point in the growth process has a lot to do with how we will relate to those who are of a different race.

DIFFERENT STROKES FOR DIFFERENT FOLKS

All of us go through stages of growth. What we need at one stage will differ greatly from what we need at another stage of our lives. So also it is in relationships. The type and quality of relationships I have as a child also will differ greatly from the type and quality of relationships I have as an adult. As we seek to relate to one another more effectively, it is essential that we be aware of the stage of identity development that person is in so that we can understand his perspective and relate to him effectively.

We must be careful not to try and relate to all minority people or all majority people in the same stereotypical manner. That's both unfair and less effective, for every man is a unique individual with his own beliefs, values, attitudes, and behaviors; those distinctions make him unique within his culture and race. Though race and culture are a part of who we are, they are not *all* of who we are as people.

Therefore, we must have a basic understanding of the stage of identity development for both minority men and white men. One way you and I can improve our ability to develop solid relationships across racial lines is by giving that person what he needs at a certain point in his development. This requires that we better understand the stages of minority development. In addition, understanding the stages of identity development will help us not to take it too personally when a brother chooses not to proceed beyond a certain level of relationship.

This chapter is primarily to help the white reader who's part of the majority understand men of color around you. But the chapter also will help those of you who are members of a minority group to recognize who you are and where you are (or should be) headed for a complete and healthy identity as a man. (In the next chapter we will look at the stages of identity development in the majority culture.)

STAGES OF MINORITY DEVELOPMENT

Three researchers have developed a model of identity development and growth that can help us better understand how our identities develop as white and non-white Americans. Called the Racial/Cultural Identity Development Model (RCID), it defines five stages of development that minority people go through as they struggle to understand themselves in terms of their own culture, the white culture (dominant culture), and the very tense relationship between the two cultures.[1]

At this point we have to use a little academic jargon. Researchers into RCID have found five stages in development: conformity, dissonance, resistance/immersion, introspection, and integrative awareness. We will explain each. Along the way you will see that key beliefs and attitudes are an integral part of the minority person's identity. Those beliefs and attitudes influence how a man views himself, others of the same minority group, others from *another* minority, and whites, who, of course, comprise the majority culture. Let's take a look at these stages in order to understand our identities—who you are, who I am.

Conformity Stage

The first stage that a minority person experiences on the road to understanding and accepting himself and his group is conformity. He views the majority culture's values and beliefs as superior to his own; in fact, he devalues his own race's values and beliefs. Constantly bombarded on all sides by reminders that whites and their way of life are superior and all other lifestyles inferior, many minorities wonder whether they themselves are not somehow inadequate or are to blame. They then begin to feel that maybe subordination and segregation are justified.

As noted in earlier chapters, the inferior status of minorities, especially their men, is constantly reinforced and perpetuated by the mass media through television, movies, newspapers, radio, books, and magazines. Such negative portrayals cause widespread harm to the self-esteem of minorities, who may incorporate them. They have become self-fulfilling prophecies: believing what they hear about themselves, they go out and fulfill those predictions.

The incorporation of the larger society's standards may lead minority-group members to react negatively toward their own racial and cultural heritage. They may become ashamed of who they are, reject their own group identification and attempt to identify with the desirable "good White majority."[2]

How does this conformity affect the minority in regard to themselves, others of the same group, others of a different minority group, and the white (majority) culture? The three researchers, Atkinson, Morten, and Sue, found the following characteristics:

1. *Attitude and beliefs toward self: racial self-hatred.* The individual will put himself down and see his physical characteristics or skin color as an impediment and a negative—a handicap. He will have low self-esteem and attempt to be as "white" as possible, hoping it will be enough to cover up his minority status.

2. *Attitudes and beliefs toward the same minority group: negative and stereotypical beliefs about his own people.* He will see "*them*" as lazy and inferior. Little thought or validity is given to other viewpoints, such as unemployment being a function of job discrimination, prejudice, racism, unequal opportunities, and inferior education.

3. *Attitudes and beliefs toward members of different minorities: in a word—discriminatory.* He regards others through his own prism of discrimination. Minority groups that are most similar to white cultural groups are viewed more favorably, whereas those most different are viewed less favorably. As Sue and Sue note:

   > For example, Asian Americans may be viewed more favorably than Blacks or Hispanics in some situations. While a stratification probably exists, we caution readers that such a ranking is fraught with hazards and potential political consequences. Such distinctions often manifest themselves in debates as to which group is more oppressed and which has done better than the others.[3]

4. *Attitudes and beliefs toward the majority culture: everything from the white culture is right.* There is then the belief that the closer I get to white (in appearance and mannerisms), the better I am as a person. The white majority can do little wrong, for they have the power, influence, and approval of American culture.

If this is where a minority man is in his identity development, what can you as a white brother do to help him move along to a mature identity? The answer can be told in the story of my friend Bill.

Years ago I held all the above attitudes. As an African-American, I sought to not talk "black" and adhered strongly to the belief that the more I was like whites the better I would be. I took great pains to perform with excellence, hoping that my black part would not be seen. The only problem was that I suffered bouts of depression because I was using a great amount of energy to cover up the fact that I was (and am) black. I never felt secure and was often angry.

This went on for a long time until Bill saw my dilemma. Bill, who is white, became a very good friend when I lived in Houston, Texas. Every time he saw me, he would celebrate my being black. He saw it as an asset—not a liability.

One Sunday I had the opportunity to preach for Bill's pastor. After speaking at Bill's church, I went to my friend's house for dinner. As we were chatting, he came over to where I was sitting and put his hands on my shoulders. Looking me in the eyes Bill said, "Rod, I thank God for your blackness—I celebrate it and am glad for how it enriches our relationship. Why don't you thank Him for it too, because your being black is not a mistake."

I broke down in tears and began to weep out loud. Finally, I was being fully accepted for all of me. I did not have to cover up anymore. I knelt and thanked God and have since then proudly proclaimed my being black. I came out of depression and moved on from there.

The best thing you can do as a white man for a minority man in this stage is to celebrate the minority man's heritage and model a positive attitude toward the minority man's culture, celebrating its equality and not reinforcing to him that it is inferior.

Dissonance Stage

"One can keep all the ping-pong balls under water for only so long before they start popping up all over the place." That's what happens in stage two. There comes a point in a minority person's life where he can no longer be in denial about his own cultural heritage. He will encounter information or experiences that will be inconsistent with culturally held beliefs, attitudes, and values. This creates dissonance—an uncomfortable tension between experiences and deceptions, reality and delusion.

Though I am part Cherokee Indian, part Anglo, and part African-American, I was taught to call myself African-American. There is another saying: "If you have one drop of black in you—then you are black." No matter how well I performed by white standards, I discovered that I wasn't quite good enough when it came to dating or other social encounters.

My denial began to break down, and I began to question and challenge attitudes/beliefs I had held during the conformity stage. This was a gradual stage for me as I began to encounter experience after experience telling me that I was not quite good enough to be considered equal.

This growing awareness typically affects the person's attitudes and beliefs four ways:

1. *The minority man feels conflict between putting himself down and appreciating his racial heritage.* There is a growing sense of personal awareness that racism does exist and that not all aspects of the minority or majority culture are good or bad. Entering into the minority person's awareness is the possibility that there are positive attributes of being from a minority culture. Feelings of shame and pride are mixed, and conflict develops in the individual.

    At this stage a key personal question is being asked, "Why should I feel ashamed of who I am?"

2. *The minority person begins to celebrate aspects of the culture he has tried to deny.* He also begins to question the majority culture's values and beliefs as being the "right" way to do things. Thus his attitudes and beliefs toward members of the same minority begin to change.

3. *His attitudes and beliefs change toward members of a different minority.* Stereotypes associated with other minority groups become questioned. The minority man senses a greater sense of comradeship with other oppressed groups.

4. *The minority person begins shifting his attitudes and beliefs toward members of the majority group.* He begins to recognize that not all of the cultural values of the majority culture are inclusive or beneficial for them. When the minority person experiences personal discrimination, he or she begins to develop a sense of distrust of the majority culture.

How do you connect with a minority man in this stage? Do not become defensive if he begins to become somewhat angry and to question the majority culture's value system. The best thing you can do to help this person is to allow him to question and affirm himself in his own cultural heritage. Do not be hesitant to talk about key figures in black history such as Martin Luther King, Jr., as well as modern-day contributors such as Jesse Jackson. Now, you may disagree with the politics of Jesse Jackson, *but* you can agree with the fact that he is trying to address some of the injustices, even though you may not agree with *how* he is doing it. The same approach—recognizing unique contributions by their forebearers to American history—can be done for Asians, Hispanics, and Native Americans.

Also, affirm the fact that the system is not always fair. Ask the brother to share his hurt and his sorrow over the experiences of discrimination with you. This way he sees you as a person and not as a part of the system. This happened to some extent during the fiftieth anniversary observances of World War II, as Japanese-Americans asked white friends and white-dominated media to remember their suffering in internment camps on the West Coast and discrimination throughout the Southwest. To simply say that's a past injustice or that you weren't there is not to acknowledge that part of his heritage.

Help this person self-explore. Ask him questions about his family life, what they liked and did not like, and where he grew up. Ask him also about his hobbies and favorite foods. Try to get to a personal level so that there is a feeling of an alliance rather than a debate.

Finally, affirm his identity in Jesus Christ. Stress to him that he is a brother in Christ and part of a new family—the family of God—and that as brothers we are committed to one another's struggles. Emphasize that God sees him as "fearfully and wonderfully" made and is committed to his well-being. God says, "I know the plans that I have for you . . . to give you a future and a hope" (Jeremiah 29:11 NASB). This is what must be emphasized when a minority man is in this stage.

Resistance and Immersion Stage

During the resistance and immersion stage, a minority person will be feeling three emotions: (1) guilt, (2) shame, and (3) anger. He is very angry and sees the majority culture not only as the problem for his dilemma but also as the enemy. He is angry because of the continued oppression he sees taking place on his people. Desire to eliminate oppression of the individual's minority group will become the key focus. He also will feel guilt and shame because of the feeling of having "sold out" to the system that has oppressed his people.

This stage affects his attitudes and beliefs four ways:

1. *He begins to celebrate his culture and background.* He may begin to wear his native dress and point out how many contributions his culture has made to this society. I remember when I was going through this stage in seminary. I began to wear an Afro. (This was pretty hard considering I was balding and had very thin and fine hair.) I found myself arguing many points in class. I would ask, "How does this fit within a minority person's context?" Often I would get blank stares or an "I don't know" answer. Sometimes I went to the extreme of pointing out the benefits of the values of the minority culture and the oppressive negatives of the majority culture.

2. *He desires and feels a strong sense of connectedness, identification, and commitment* with other members of his particular racial and cultural group. Cultural values of the minority group are accepted without question—there is almost a glorification of those values. A minority man in this stage is likely to restrict his interactions as much as possible to members of his own group.

3. *He joins in alliances with other minorities.* There is a growing sense of comradeship with persons from other minority groups. Yet there is a strong sense of adhering to one's own culture and issues.

4. *He regards the majority group with growing distrust, which soon becomes disdain.* The majority culture is seen, quite frankly, as the enemy. There is a feeling of distrust and dislike for all members of the majority group. Considerable anger and hostility are expressed in this stage because the white majority are seen as the oppressors.

As a member of the majority—a majority that has become pictured as the enemy during this stage—how *can* you relate to a minority man in this stage?

First, recognize that as a white man you may be viewed as a *symbol* of the oppressive establishment. *Do not* become defensive and personalize the attacks. Do not be intimidated or afraid of the anger. Allow the person to vent. Try to look beyond the anger and see the hurt and pain he is going through.

In addition, expect to be tested concerning your willingness, openness, and commitment to the relationship. Hang in there when arguments get heated or tough—do not quit coming back.

Finally, speak the truth in love. Recognize the injustices of the system, but remind the minority man that *you* are not the system—you are his friend. Focus on what is left, not on what is lost. Celebrate what you have together in Christ.

A group of six white brothers got me through this stage. I mentioned earlier how I had experienced racism while I was a seminary student. After enduring subtle racism on campus, I had become almost militant in my classes and conversations. I was *angry*. I lived in the dorm, and soon had the nickname "the bear" because of the disposition I had when interacting with the people around me. Instead of being pleasant and outgoing, I became sullen and argumentative. I would make almost every argument a "racial" argument: "Yeah, well that sounds like a white perspective to me."

When my friends would try to reach out to me I would say, "I have to study." Sometimes in anger, I just exclaimed, "Look, just leave me alone."

I had six white friends at this time, but I began to distance myself from them as well. I quit coming to our weekly Bible study and would go out of my way to not interact with them.

This went on for weeks, the separation obviously getting wider. Then one night I was walking down the hall toward my room, when a door opened and a hand reached out and pulled me inside. I found myself sitting on a chair surrounded by my six friends.

"Rod, we do not know what is happening to you," one of the guys began, "but if you were to graduate from here today, you couldn't minister to a rock, let alone people. Tell us what is wrong, let us help you. You are not leaving until we get this straightened out."

I exploded in anger. "Who are you to tell me to change—*you people* are the problem."

"We are your *friends*," he said simply. "Through thick and thin, we love you, man. Help us to help you."

I broke down in tears and began to sob. I told them about how I had this fantasy that seminary would be a place where I would be *totally* accepted by *all* people.

"Some students here belittle my culture. They make snide remarks about black preachers on TV and radio and imply that they were good preachers but had no content. When ministry is discussed in classes it always centers around a white middle-class perspective. It never seems to include my people."

Then I told them how I was angry about not being seen as an individual but often being related to as a stereotype. It seemed that when guys would approach me they would change their speech and mannerisms, trying to "relate" instead of being themselves and letting me be myself.

We all cried together and prayed together. One of my six friends said, "Hey, Rod, we just want to get to know you and learn from you." They let me know how they valued me and asked forgiveness if they had come across in a way that belittled me. They let me know that they were on my side and just wanted to be my friends.

I left that room not a *bitter* man—but a *better* man. You see, they loved *me* and showed me that they were not part of the system but part of the solution. This event helped me to get to the fourth stage.

Introspection Stage

The fourth stage, introspection, tends to be a reaction against the majority culture. The individual becomes reactive rather than proactive in finding his identity. For instance, in the African-American community he may call another brother an "Oreo" (black on the outside but white on the inside). Or he may receive the label by a reactionary brother calling for separation or distinction from the white majority culture.

The minority person sometimes feels that he is in a "no man's land" because he doesn't feel he quite fits anywhere. At one time he may be strongly defending his own race and at other times may find himself saying to a black brother that he needs to take responsibility and move on.

He is trying to evaluate his next step. During this stage he begins to recognize that he also is an individual with individual attitudes and beliefs, which at times comes into conflict with his own racial group's beliefs and attitudes. During my introspection stage, for instance, I was asked by some of my African-American friends to not associate with some of my white friends because they were the enemy. However, my personal experiences did not fully support their view. I began to realize I needed to make individual choices that would at times not be popular with the group.

The conflicts that occur during the introspection stage affect four areas of a minority's attitudes and beliefs:

1. *With self: balance begins to take place for the minority person.* There is a need to continue to support one's own ethnic group, but at the same time personal goals and responsibilities must be pursued. Conflict occurs from trying to be an individual

and support the group as well. Sometimes what the individual is called to may not fit with the aspirations of the group.

2. *Toward members of the same minority: the minority man no longer sees the majority culture as all "bad" and the minority culture as all "good."* Increasingly, he may see his group taking positions that seem rather extreme. Also, he may become angry at his own group for trying to pressure him into being conformed to their desires as opposed to allowing him to form his own convictions.

3. *Toward members of a different minority: a movement takes place where there is a greater need in understanding the plight of others and their unique struggles.*

4. *Attitudes toward the majority culture: balance is again the key.* Here the person tries to discern what elements from his own culture and the majority culture fit best for him. Benefits from the majority culture are acknowledged, but the minority man wants to make sure he is not selling out his own culture to achieve those benefits.

How does one relate to a minority man in this stage? The best way to help is to help him not to have an "all or none" mentality. He needs to see that both "good and bad" elements exist in both the majority and minority culture. Help him see that to adhere to some of the values of the majority culture is not "selling out" to the culture. Also, a majority man can point him to further clarifying what is biblical and what is cultural.

Integrative Awareness Stage

The fifth and final stage is called integrative awareness. At this point the minority man has developed an inner sense of security and can now appreciate unique aspects of his own culture as well as the majority culture. He now believes that there are acceptable and unacceptable aspects in all cultures, and he has discerned what is biblical and what is cultural. At this stage, the minority man wants to eliminate oppression for *all people,* regardless of color.

In stage five he has come full circle, and he is comfortable with his identity as a minority person living in a majority culture. Consider his attitudes in the following four areas:

1. *Toward self: he has a strong sense of confidence and self-worth.* He is a multicultural person in that "he perceives himself as an autonomous individual who is unique (individual level of identity), a member of one's own racial-cultural group (group level of identity), a member of a larger society, and a member of the human race (universal level of identity).[4] I would also add that he has a primary recognition that he is a child of God first, and his primary objective is to build the kingdom of God.

2. *Toward members of the same group: he has a strong sense of appreciation for his own group's contributions and certain values,* but not all of them. There is a strong sense of empathy concerning the group's experiences, coupled with an awareness that each person carries responsibility as an individual.

3. *Toward members of different minorities: he is reaching out to understand and connect on deeper levels to other minority groups.* He has a desire to know more about others and be enriched by them.

4. *Toward members of the majority culture: he has a selective appreciation.* The minority man no longer sees white people as the enemy but views them as individuals who also are at various stages in their growth. He has an openness to close relationships with whites and a realization that white racism is a sickness in society and that whites are also victims who are in as much need of help to break free from the system as minority people are.

Reconciliation and relationships cut both ways. Attempts to reach out must be made on the part of the white man to the minority man and vice versa. If you are a non-white man, keep in mind that whites also go through stages of identity development before they are able to accept themselves and to realize that racism exists in the lives of fellow white Americans and often even in themselves. They move through stages that culminate in their own integrative awareness stage, a stage that affirms the part of his culture that is nonexploiting, while acknowledging the existence of racism and working toward its eradication. In the next chapter we'll look at those five stages and give suggestions to minority men for helping white men as they move through those stages.

TAKE ACTION

1. How has your perspective on racial issues changed in the last twenty years? In what ways do you anticipate change today? In the next five years? Assess in your own life what is left, not what is lost.

2. As a minority person, in which stage of development are you? What examples can you give from your own life that represent each stage? Where are your brothers in the stages of development? How can you best support them?

3. If you are a majority person, which of the suggestions are the most helpful to you in relating to a minority man in one of these stages? Determine to put a couple of them into effect in the next month.

CHAPTER NINE
A White Man's Identity

I f you are feeling sorry, or even angry, that minority men undergo a multistage process of developing and accepting their distinctive identity, keep in mind that they are not alone. The majority American culture—white and predominantly Anglo Saxon—also goes through a five-step development process in search of its identity. It is part of the cost of having a racial divide in America. Racism, though subtle, is present in almost every white American, and it has left its mark on a white man's identity. It's a major reason Christian men of every color must seek reconciliation with one another. Only in this way can we achieve our intended, whole identities as men created in God's image.

Whites go through the identical stages in their identity development that we saw in the previous chapter, with slightly different consequences than those for non-white men. Therefore this chapter helps minority men to better understand the attitudes and actions of the majority white culture, as white men seek to accept their identity. It also will help white men recognize where they may be in identity development.

THE WHITE ADVANTAGE

Recently several multicultural experts in the field have emphasized the need to deal with concepts of whiteness and white development. Derald Wing Sue and David Sue have studied various models of white development. Though differences exist, they have found that the various models of white identity development share some key assumptions:

> First, racism is a basic and integral part of the U.S. life and permeates all aspects of our culture and institutions. Second, Whites are socialized into U.S. society and, therefore, inherit the biases, stereotypes, and racist attitudes of the society. Third, *how Whites perceive themselves as racial beings seems to follow an identifiable sequence that can be called stages.* Fourth, the stage of White Racial Identity development in a cross-cultural encounter affects the process and outcome of an interracial relationship.
>
> Last, the most desirable stage is the one where the White person not only accepts his/her Whiteness, but defines it in a nondefensive and nonracist manner.[1] (emphasis added)

Notice the emphasized third point. It seems that white men go through stages that almost parallel the minority experience. If you are a minority man, recognize that a white person is in a closed system as you are. He has been socialized into playing his role as well. *I believe that no child is born wanting to be a racist.* Instead he is taught to see his world as the privileged and the best. He is unaware of his bias. We must recognize that whites *do* benefit from the majority position in our culture—and white men need to acknowledge that position of advantage as well. In this area white men and women must be open and honest and be willing to even the playing field.

STAGES OF MAJORITY DEVELOPMENT

Here are the five stages of identity development for whites that a minority man (and a white man) must be aware of in forming interracial relationships.

Conformity Stage

The white person's attitudes and beliefs during the conformity stage are one dimensional. He has little awareness of being in a distinct ethnic group—white. His key belief is in the superiority of white culture and the inferiority of minority culture. Stereotypes dominate this person's thinking. Consciously or unconsciously, he sees whiteness as a privilege. "The conformity stage is often marked by contradictory and often compartmentalized attitudes, beliefs, and behaviors."[2]

This person may not see himself as a racist. He believes that minority people are deviant and different but proclaims that "people are people" and differences are unimportant. This attitude keeps the white person in denial and allows the white person to avoid personal responsibility.

A white youth leader in a church in Denver said he enjoyed watching his predominantly white high school youth group accept a challenge to invite teenagers from a predominantly African-American part of town to participate in basketball (and on some nights volleyball) and then join them in a group Bible study. A couple of African-American teenagers came and discovered that they were well accepted and had a great time. The next time the white youth group met, several more African-American youth came, and, before long, the high school group was almost half African-American and half white.

At first, one of the elders who worked with the youth leader thought it was a good idea because "people are people." Yet, as the numbers of the minority youth grew, the elder felt that the values and beliefs of the black youth were not compatible with the church and maybe "they" should start their own group. The elder couched his concern in saying things like he just wanted to be "culturally sensitive."

How does a minority person relate to a white man in this stage? Follow the biblical mandate of "speaking the truth in love" to this person. When I was attending seminary, many of my white brothers were in this stage, and I found myself getting quite angry. I went to one professor with whom I felt safe to share my anger, Howard Hendricks (now you know the seminary). He gave me some sage advice: "Rod, as a black evangelical, you will have to learn to laugh a lot, because if you do not, you will always be angry at us. Sometimes, son, we just do not know how to relate."

We must be willing to point out various attitudes and comments that hurt us as minority men, but we also must recognize that this is a process. We must be consistent in our efforts to educate with the hope that our white brothers will be willing to "have ears to hear."

Dissonance Stage

The dissonance stage occurs when the white person is willing to deal with the inconsistencies that have been compartmentalized when dealing with minority people. A white person at this stage recognizes his "whiteness" and begins to examine his own cultural values and sees the conflict between upholding nonracist attitudes and their own contradictory behavior. He may begin to see how "the system" acts in favor of whites and oppresses minorities.

This is a risky stage because to begin to speak up about racism may put the white person at risk with his own peer group.

> Feelings of guilt, shame, anger, and depression may characterize this stage. Guilt and shame may be associated with the recognition of the White person's role in perpetuating racism in the past. Or, guilt may result from the person's being afraid to speak out on the issues or to take responsibility for his/her part in a current situation.[3]

For instance, a person may hear a racist comment or be given preferential treatment over a minority person but does not speak up for fear of being ostracized by his or her own group. This is a crucial stage for a white person. He will either retreat back to the conformity stage with the attitude "I'm just one person—what can I do about it?" or he will begin to honestly look at the discrepancies between being white and being a minority in America.

How does a minority man relate to men in the majority culture at this stage? Be patient, pray for them, and continue to speak the truth in love. Research shows that it is only through relationships that attitudes change. As a minority man, do not give up. Hang in there and be patient.

Resistance/Immersion Stage

In the resistance/immersion stage the white person has the "A-ha" experience. It's a time of discovery, of revelation. He begins to recognize the racism around him. The advertisements, movies, television, even educational materials proclaim a white racial superiority, and he begins to recognize this racism. The white person also begins to experience anger and guilt for having been a part of a system oppressive to minorities. There also may be a sense of shame regarding the "white race" as a whole.

The white person at this stage may try to overidentify with minorities or devote his energies toward protecting minorities. Neither is a good strategy. This is where the white person must sort out what is good about his own culture and what has to change.

I know some white brothers who entered this stage during the the Rodney King controversy. After the Los Angeles black motorist was beaten by police and the police officers were found innocent of using unnecessary force, several white male colleagues came to me to express their sorrow over the verdict. These brothers were truly angry and ashamed of what their "race" had done in this incident. That was the beginning of some excellent dialogue between us as to how to begin to address racism on our own seminary campus and among ourselves.

You would expect that on a seminary campus where relationships had been building between myself and my colleagues there would be this kind of response to the King verdict. Yet I discovered that there was this same response by whites citywide and nationwide. I was at a restaurant and overheard several whites, without blacks being in their presence, say how appalled they were at the verdict and "No wonder black people feel paranoid when such obvious injustices are done." In the award-winning book *Breaking Down Walls,* Raleigh Washington writes,

> Several white members in our church approached me ... and other blacks in the congregation and said, "When I heard that decision I was ashamed that I am white." They saw the verdict as evil, and as part of the white race they grieved the jury's decision. They accepted responsibility for the decision even though they did not participate directly in it.[4]

I was encouraged to see that the response to the King verdict was appalling to many whites in various circles, and this gave me hope.

How does a minority man relate to a white brother during this stage? Do not put blame and shame on our brother in this stage. He already feels the sting of guilt for having personally or corporately as a race contributed to the oppression of minorities. This is a time of forgiveness and reconciliation. This is a time when we focus not on what is lost but on what is left. Now meaningful dialogue can begin to take place as to how to address the injustices of racism. Also, celebrate and affirm the white brother in his willingness to bring about change.

Introspective Stage

During the introspective stage the white person begins to ask the serious question, "What is biblical, and what is cultural?" Here an independent search for goals and direction beyond merely reacting to white racism is needed. The white person in this stage no longer denies that he is white; he lessens his defensive attitude and guilt associated with being white.

How does a minority person relate to the white person going through this stage? If you desire to be a friend, you will, as a minority man, listen to his questions as he undertakes the search. You will be there as a sounding board and guide for the white brother. Help him to come up with goals that fit him and his talents in bridging the gap of racism. Also, help him to celebrate his ethnicity as well and not to have an all or none attitude about being white.

A black friend I'll call Alan is married to Jill, who is white. He met Jill at a Bible college, and when they announced their engagement to her family there was some surprise as well as resistance, especially on the part of the future father-in-law. The father-in-law, James, came from a strong German background and was a farmer in Nebraska, where the only exposure to blacks was the University of Nebraska's football team. Even though he felt he was open biblically, he knew he was having a hard time with his daughter marrying a black man.

Alan recognized that his future father-in-law was uncomfortable, so he decided to go with Jill to her dad's home so that James and he could get to know each other. Alan went on several visits, and as Alan worked on the farm and as he shared about himself and his values, the two men slowly began to build a relationship. His father-in-law's commitment to biblical values and willingness to learn allowed them to get to know each other.

Alan, Jill, and James also went to his future father-in-law's all-white church as a family. They did this only after James felt comfortable with my friend. There was quite a stir in the church over my friend's presence and future marriage to one of their members, yet the father-in-law began to introduce my friend as his future son-in-law.

The upshot of the story is that Alan now is great friends with his father-in-law and is often asked to preach in their church when he goes to James's home. Because of his father-in-law's commitment to what is biblical, he slowly changed his actions to match his beliefs. Alan did not try to go deep quickly; he began slowly on his father-in-law's turf and built the relationship to where his father-in-law's fears dissipated, and he got to know him as a person. His father-in-law now does not see race as an obstacle but as an enrichment to their family.

Integrative Awareness Stage

During the integrative awareness stage, a white person has a solid racial/cultural identity. He begins to truly affirm that part of his culture that is nonexploiting and character building. He no longer denies personal responsibility for perpetuating racism and is not immobilized by guilt. He has an increased awareness of how the "system" works and how it affects race relations, an increased appreciation for cultural diversity (different is just different—not inferior or superior), and a solid commitment toward the eradication of racism.

One Hispanic friend of mine put it well when he said, "We are truly friends when I feel comfortable enough to go to your house, open the refrigerator and get something to drink or eat without asking, and you can feel that same freedom when you come to my house as well. We have truly become friends." A minority man treats the white brother as that—another one of the family. We may have disagreements, but there is a loyalty that supersedes the problems. There is a feeling that we are family.

I taught a graduate school class for several years on cross-cultural counseling. Most of the time, more than 90 percent of my students were white, and during each class I watched them go through these stages. Admittedly, not every student went all the way through them. But invariably, by the end of the class, many of the students are giving me articles or alerting me to various ways our society is promoting racism. But what encouraged me most was when those students told me they no longer were willing to be a part of the *system* but wanted to be part of the *solution*.

What brought about the change in these students? What are the necessary ingredients for truly achieving the integrative awareness stage and racial reconciliation? For both the white majority and the racial minorities, three key ingredients lead to stage five and to a willingness to accept one's own responsibility for developing friendships across the cultures.

In our final chapter we will look at those three ingredients that lead to an acceptance of self and those of other races and to a desire to develop cross-cultural relationships. Such relationships help us on the way to racial reconciliation. You have come this far; keep reading to find out how to begin the journey for racial reconciliation.

TAKE ACTION

1. As a white person, in which stage of development are you? What examples can you give from your own life that represent each stage? Where are your brothers in the stages of development? How can you best support them?

2. If you are a minority person, which of the suggestions are the most helpful to you in relating to a minority man in one of these stages? Determine to put a couple of them into effect in the next month.

3. In what ways can you celebrate your own culture? The culture of your brother? What can you and your brother do to celebrate your common identities in Christ? List several of these actions you can take, and then make specific plans to act on that list.

CHAPTER TEN
More Than a Dream

I t was an amazing sight in front of the Lincoln Memorial on August 28, 1963. More than 200,000 persons had participated in a "march for jobs and freedom" in Washington, D.C., and now gathered in front of the famous monument to hear speakers call for equal opportunity and employment for all races. The marchers, concerned with issues of civil rights and poverty, had come from all walks of life, from labor leaders and politicians, to students and teachers, rich and poor, black and white. Finally they listened as Martin Luther King, Jr., president of the Southern Christian Leadership Conference, came to the podium to tell them about his dream.

Dr. King's "I Have a Dream" speech will go down in history as one of the great messages on racial reconciliation. The crowd roared as King reached his stirring conclusion, when he told of his dream of being able to say one day: "Free at last, free at last, thank God Almighty, I am free at last." Those closing words today remain the most celebrated part of his speech. Yet the beginning of the speech also contained some powerful words:

> When the architects of our republic wrote the magnificent words of the Constitution and the Declaration of Independence, they were signing a promissory note to which every American was to fall heir. This note was a promise that all men would be guaranteed the unalienable rights of life, liberty, and the pursuit of happiness.

It is obvious today that America has defaulted on this promissory note insofar as her citizens of color are concerned. Instead of honoring this sacred obligation, America has given the Negro people a bad check marked "insufficient funds." But we refuse to believe that the bank of justice is bankrupt. We refuse to believe that there are insufficient funds in the great vaults of opportunity of this nation. So we have come to cash this check—a check that will give us upon demand the riches of freedom and the security of justice.

We have also come to this hallowed spot to remind America of the fierce urgency of NOW. This is no time to engage in the luxury of cooling off or to take the tranquilizing drug of gradualism. NOW is the time to make real the promises of democracy. NOW is the time to arise from the dark and desolate valley of segregation to the sunlit path of racial justice. NOW is the time to open the doors of opportunity to all of God's children. NOW is the time to lift our nation from the quicksands of racial injustice to the solid rock of brotherhood.[1]

Three decades ago King delivered this speech with the belief that America was founded and operated upon biblical principles. This was not just a racial issue but also a biblical and moral one. The guiding principle of King's speech would fit well with the apostle James's statement in James 4:17: "One who knows the right thing to do, and does not do it, to him it is sin" (NASB).

"YOU ARE ALL ONE"

I believe that racial reconciliation and brotherhood are more than a dream. I believe that the "brotherhood" King talked about in principle can be experienced in real life for those of us who are God's children. We cannot legislate "brotherhood." A good friend of mine, E. V. Hill, once told me, "Rod, don't put your trust in the right wing or the left wing when the bird is dead." The system that keeps us locked into our roles can only change because of a people who are changed on the inside. The apostle Paul wrote,

You are all sons of God through faith in Christ Jesus, for all of you who were baptized into Christ have clothed yourselves with Christ. There is neither Jew nor Greek, slave nor free, male nor female, for you are all one in Christ Jesus. If you belong to Christ, then you are Abraham's seed, and heirs according to the promise. (Galatians 3:26–29; see also 4:1–7)

Paul is telling us that we have all been enslaved to a world that operates on pride, power, and distinctions. I call it a closed system (see chapter 1). Jesus has redeemed us from a closed system so that we might truly experience freedom as brothers in the family of God. Jesus Himself said,

> You know that the rulers of the Gentiles lord it over them, and their high officials exercise authority over them. Not so with you. Instead, whoever wants to become great among you must be your servant, and whoever wants to be first must be your slave—just as the Son of Man did not come to be served, but to serve, and to give His life as a ransom for many. (Matthew 20:25–28)

As Christian men, we have the same heritage (we are Abraham's seed), we are sons (we have the same Redeemer and Father), and we have the same Spirit, which means we have been enabled to live as brothers, and the same mandate—to be servants to one another. Truly, our sonship in Christ transcends culture and evens the playing field, for there is now "neither Jew nor Greek."

THE ANSWER ACCORDING TO MICAH

But you might be saying, "Well, Rod, that is great theology, but how do we work this out in our relationships and daily living?"

I believe that the answer for racial reconciliation is quite simple, but that does not mean it is easy. The answer for us is simply laid out by a lesser known prophet of the Old Testament, Micah. Listen to Micah's words: "He has told you, O Man, what is good; and what does the Lord require of you but to do justice, to love kindness, and to walk humbly with your God?" (6:8 NASB).

The prophet Micah was writing to a group of people who were willing to do all sorts of religious things for God but were not willing to do what was *needful*. He reminded the people of Judah that they had made a covenant to be faithful to God and His desires.

Micah was exposing the injustice of Judah and the righteousness and justice of God. About one-third of the book chastises Israel and Judah for specific sins, especially those of oppression and exploitation of the powerless. Another third of the book predicts the judgment that will come because of those sins. The rest of the book is a message of hope and consolation. Micah pointed out that true peace and justice would prevail only when the Messiah reigned and they, as a people, committed themselves to live out the covenant made to God and to one another.

The key to Micah is the strong integral relationship between true spirituality and true ethics. When Jesus Christ reigns in our hearts, we can experience solid relationships with each other because of our relationship to Him.

Micah 6:8 summarizes what God wants to see in His people: justice and equity tempered with mercy and compassion, which flows from a humble and obedient relationship with Him. You see, God does not want any thing from us—He wants us.

God is not requiring some religious ritual but certain qualities of the heart: righteousness, love, and humility. In fact, the lifestyle that God approves of consists of three elements: a strict adherence to that which is equitable in all dealings with our fellow brothers; a heart determined to do them good; and diligent care to live in close intimate fellowship with God.

Whether you are black, white, brown, red, or yellow, the path to racial reconciliation passes through the gates of Micah 6:8. Now that we know what God desires, what does it look like to do justice, to love kindness, and to walk humbly with your God?

"TO DO JUSTICE"

What does it mean "to do justice"? Among the several definitions of *justice* in Webster's New World Dictionary are the following: (1) being righteous, (2) fairness, (3) righteousness, and (4) the use of authority to uphold what is just. There is also the phrase "do justice to," which is defined as "to treat fairly or with due appreciation." But in order to "do" justice, one must first of all "be" just. I have found that in order to do justice one must go through a three-step process: confession, repentance, and restitution.

Confession

Confession means telling the truth and acknowledging the unjust or hurtful actions of myself or my ancestors toward other people or people groups. The first part of doing justice is admitting that a wrong has been committed. Usually, at this point, I hear my white brothers saying, "But it is not my fault. I was not the one who made your people slaves." It is at this point that I hear my African-American brothers saying, "Forget it. It's no use."

Derald Sue and David Sue point out two key assumptions on which a minority man operates. One is that "most Whites are racist and [the] second is that most Whites find such a concept disturbing and will go to great lengths to deny they are racist or biased." They add: "Some of this is done deliberately with awareness, but in most cases one's racism is largely unconscious."[2]

When I hear my white brothers say, "I had nothing to do with slavery even though it was wrong," the minority man tends to remember the part that says, "It wasn't my fault." Rightly or wrongly a minority man puts up his guard and sees the above assumptions being fulfilled. So there is no further contact.

One African-American friend told me that when a white brother says, "I am sorry for what my people have done," it tells the minority man that he is willing to do whatever it takes to make it right.

In admitting our racial sins of prejudice, we must accept responsibility for what others did in the past. We bear responsibility *now.* Confession is a humbling act. You are admitting that you have acted in a wrong manner against one minority or another, either in thought or deed. Blacks against Asians, Asians against blacks, Hispanics against American Indians, etc. And whites, as the majority, have alienated most minority groups with their presumption of having a better way and unconscious attitude of racial superiority. We *all* need to admit our sins in avoiding one another.

The Bible indicates that we are sinners corporately. Romans 5:12 says, "Sin entered the world through one man, and death through sin, and in this way death came to all men, because all sinned." So it is not a stretch for us to be corporately responsible for what our ancestors have done to others. For instance, Nehemiah petitioned God, "[Lord], let your ear be attentive and your eyes open to hear the prayer your servant is praying before you day and night for your servants, the people of Israel. *I confess the sins we Israelites, including myself and my father's house, have committed against you*" (1:6–7; emphasis added). The prophet Daniel also understood this principle of joint accountability for sins:

> We have not obeyed the Lord our God or kept the laws he gave us through his servants the prophets. All Israel has transgressed your law and turned away, refusing to obey you . . . . Our sins and the iniquities of our fathers have made Jerusalem and your people an object of scorn to all those around us. (9:10–16b)

Daniel confessed his sin on behalf of the Hebrew people, even though he personally did not commit the sin.

Nehemiah and Daniel took personal responsibility for their ancestors even though neither personally participated in the sins being confessed. Now my white brothers usually say, "OK, I will accept re-

149

sponsibility—but what about you?" This is when my black brothers say, "Hey, we did not start this." I agree, but we must do our part not to keep it going.

Glen Kehrein, the white director of a Chicago social agency, actively sought the friendship of a black man. In his book *Breaking Down Walls*, he wrote that learning to admit his responsibility was crucial to reconciliation—as was the need for blacks to also confess their wrongful attitudes.

> Whites must admit responsibility; but blacks also must admit wrongful attitudes. I . . . found that when I began to take responsibility for racial injustice, many blacks were willing to increase my guilt. Finding a white person willing to admit racism and "see it like it is" did not always generate reconciliation—it generated more blame. I became a lightning rod for suppressed rage. Thus African-Americans must stand ready to admit their damage. Blacks feel justified to withhold trust because they have been hurt so many times. Bitterness and anger seethe under the surface for many blacks, but dumping on whites who want to change is unfair. Black Christians must have an attitude of forgiveness and stand ready to trust.[3]

Kehrein is correct. The majority man and the minority man each bear responsibility to own his part of the problem and confess it. We cannot do justice until we have the right attitudes followed by the right actions.

At times public confession will be appropriate. Author John Dawson recounted a reconciliation ceremony performed at Sand Creek, Colorado, the site of a major massacre in the 1800s against Native-American people.

Native Americans and white Christians met at Sand Creek to begin the reconciliation process. The white believers, on behalf of themselves and their ancestors, made confession and asked for forgiveness in four areas. Let me highlight two of them: injustices by the government and military, and social injustices. Here is a portion of the document signed by the white Christians:

Government—military

- Dishonest agents of the federal government, in cooperation with railroad, timber, mercantile and land speculators, defrauded the Indians of their government allotments of land and timber, cash and goods; against which the Native Americans could find no legal recourse.
- The government made and failed to enforce over three hundred treaties.

- Although there was a congressional investigation of the Sand Creek Massacre, the matter was mostly swept under the political rug, and was never satisfactorily resolved.

For the wrongs committed, for the related betrayals of your trust, and for the atrocity of Sand Creek, we offer our apology and ask for forgiveness.

Social injustices—prejudices

- Indian peoples have been subjected to numerous social injustices and prejudices. Indian children were removed from their homes in order to make them into 'white children.' Sometimes the children were never returned. These children were forbidden to speak their own language in school and were punished for it.
- The Indian people have been subjected to blatant prejudice and subservient positions in society, and we have been insensitive to the problems that confront the American Indian people today, such as 90 percent alcoholism, poor health care, lack of adequate housing, alcoholism touching 75 percent of homes, a suicide rate 5 times higher than any other ethnic group, and an average life expectancy of only 40.1 years.

We apologize for these wrongs and injustices, and ask for forgiveness.[4]

The other two areas in which wrongs were confessed were sins of missionaries and others bearing Christ's name and violation of stewardship of the land.

The Native Americans at the ceremony cried with many tears and also asked for forgiveness for the tremendous anger and bitterness they felt over the many years as well. This was the beginning of the reconciliation process. Statements of confession by members of an offending group can go far in restoring justice and moving men into the path toward reconciliation.

Repentance

The second part necessary in order to do justice is repentance. *Repentance* means turning away from unloving actions to loving actions. In repenting, the individual declares that he will not carry on or promote the stereotypes and attitudes that keep us locked into our various roles in society.

Repentance, of course, occurs first and foremost in the heart. There's a change in attitude. But repentance often expresses itself in words as well, declaring that one's past actions were wrong and pledging, with God's help, to do acts of justice.

I was encouraged when a student who loved to tell jokes revealed that he would no longer be telling racist jokes. He "turned away" from promoting stereotypes. His actions showed a repentant heart.

Restitution

Restitution is an attempt to restore that which has been damaged or destroyed and seek justice wherever we have power to act or to influence those in authority to act. Dawson tells the story of a Denver oil man, who, after the reconciliation ceremony at Sand Creek, made a proposal. He owned land in a part of Wyoming that had belonged to a particular group of Native Americans. He pointed out that he owned the natural gas rights on that land and paid a royalty to the government on every well he owned. He said that he was prepared to pay an extra royalty to the descendants of the Indians displaced by the treaty violations from this area. That happened to be a huge amount of money.[5] But the oil man paid them anyway.

You see, restitution implies obedience, whatever the cost. It means that I am willing to sacrifice my comfort zone to bring about what God desires. Talking justice is easier than doing it.

Doing justice may mean personal sacrifice as well as taking unpopular stands. Haddon Robinson, a professor, preacher, and former president of Denver Seminary, once was asked to preach at a Dallas Seminary banquet. His text was James 5:4, which says, "Look! The wages you failed to pay the workmen who mowed your fields, are crying out against you. The cries of the harvesters have reached the ears of the Lord Almighty." Robinson, my mentor, pointed out that, if a person owned a farm and paid migrant farm workers below the minimum wage for their work, they would be offending Almighty God Himself. Later, a call came to the seminary from a person in California, apparently an employer of farm workers, who said that as a result of Robinson's statement, he would no longer contribute his $200,000 a year to the school.

Sometimes doing justice can be costly. To do justice means that we must do whatever we can to show a deep appreciation for those who are different than we are. If we do justice, we are well on our way to reconciliation.

"TO LOVE KINDNESS"

To love kindness means that we are to respond to one another out of a spirit of generosity, grace, and loyalty. The Hebrew word for "kindness" is *ḥesed*. This word is especially rich in meaning because it implies a strong element of loyalty, such as that between a husband and wife or between true friends. It is used of God's continual love for Israel.

To love kindness means we have the ability to overlook faults and meet needs—to give each other the benefit of the doubt when problems arise in the relationship. It is the belief that in the other person's heart there is a desire to do the right thing, even when it is hard.

An African-American friend of mine named John recounted an incident when he was playing golf with a white buddy named Bill. John said that he was putting on some sun screen because it was a particularly sunny day. Without thinking Bill said, "I thought you folks didn't need that stuff." John related, "I felt my neck begin to stiffen, and I wanted to tell Bill about his racism. Then I thought, If this guy did not want the relationship, he would not have invited me to play golf with him at his private club."

After they had finished the round of golf, John explained to Bill how that remark was hurtful. Bill said, "I had no idea. Please forgive me, and let's start over." John also gave Bill permission to correct him if he said something that was out of line.

Howard Hendricks put it well when he told me, "Rod, being black and evangelical, you are going to have to laugh a lot, because we are going to make a lot of mistakes out of ignorance—we just do not know." Dr. Hendricks was telling me to be gracious. If we are going to have reconciliation, then we must have an attitude of kindness toward each other as we develop our relationships. Raleigh Washington and Glen Kehrein say,

> The good news is that the road map for achieving racial reconciliation has been given to the body of Christ. Racial reconciliation is more than intellectual assent to a theological concept; it's putting rubber to the road. We—Glen and Raleigh, white and black—are committed to each other as brothers in Christ for a much longer time than to our natural relatives because when we die, our human family relationships will end, but we are spiritual brothers for all of eternity. All Christians can and should have such relationships with believers of other races.[6]

Since we are brothers in Christ, may we show as much patience with each other as Christ has with us.

"TO WALK HUMBLY WITH YOUR GOD"

Flavel, a Puritan writer, once said, "A man cannot think highly of himself and God at the same time." Walking humbly with God means that we keep in the forefront of our minds that we are all sinners saved by grace. No one has a monopoly on the grace of God. To "walk humbly" with God also means to see all of life through His eyes and behave toward our brothers with the same compassion and longsuffering that God has toward us. The humility we are to have is in direct opposition to the pride and presumption that naturally drives us to be self-centered or have the need to prove our superiority over one another.

In Luke 24:13–35, we see two of Jesus' disciples walking with Him on the road to Emmaus. They did not know it was Jesus until He revealed Himself that evening at supper and then disappeared. Afterward they commented, "Were not our hearts burning within us while He was speaking to us on the road, while He was explaining the Scriptures to us?" (v. 32). Walking with God keeps in front of us an eternal perspective, a biblical view, and a continual focus of what would be pleasing to God.

Walking humbly with God also means that we are in submission to His leading. Amos says, "Do two walk together unless they have agreed to do so?" (3:3). Therefore, we are available to go where He leads and to do what He asks, whatever that might be because our Father God was willing to give whatever it took, His only Son, to bring about reconciliation.

This is the only command of the three that is directed toward God. It does not refer to self-effacement but to bringing our lives into conformity with God's will. In order to do justice and to love kindness we must walk humbly with our God. Jesus said in John 15:5: "I am the vine; you are the branches. If a man remains in me and I in him, he will bear much fruit; apart from me you can do nothing." Jesus later adds: "My command is this: Love each other as I have loved you" (v. 12). Following Jesus means loving each other.

AN ENDURING LOVE

Ever feel overwhelmed by Jesus' command to love unconditionally? When people ask me, "How can I start to love everyone like I should?" I give the same answer I give those who ask how they can start jogging: Start slow, then get slower! For the first week the goal is just to keep moving.

Too many people buy new shoes and a fancy running suit and sprint out the door, eagerly chugging as hard as they can for about three blocks. Then their stomachs begin to ache, their muscles cramp, and their lungs burn. They wind up hitchhiking home, exhausted, and gasping, "I will never do that again!" That's called anaerobic (without oxygen) running. It's caused by the body using up more oxygen than it takes in.

Many people try to run that way, and many people try to love that way. They love with great fervor and self-sacrifice, giving 100 percent but without the resources to continue for a lifetime. Down the road they find themselves in pain, gasping and cramped, saying, "I will never do that again!"

Love, like running, must be aerobic. Our output must be matched by our intake. Running requires oxygen. An enduring love requires God's Word, His consolation, His presence. As we love aerobically, we'll build up our capacity to do more and more. And pretty soon we won't be huffing and puffing for half a mile; we'll be running marathons.

The only way we can have reconciliation as brothers is if we are walking humbly with our God, staying close to Him, abiding in Him, and using His resources to have the staying power to build solid cross-cultural relationships as brothers. In Micah the message of Jesus is foreshadowed: "First be reconciled to your brother, and then come and present your offering" (Matthew 5:24). If we do justice, love kindness, and walk humbly with our God, we will be men in reconciliation.

TAKE ACTION

1. The author states that sometimes doing justice can be costly. What has your cost been? What is your attitude toward sins your ancestors committed? As a man of color, can you forgive these descendants?

2. The Sand Creek incident (page 150) is a dramatic way that the white majority did justice to Native Americans by accepting responsibility and asking forgiveness. List ways in which you can begin to do justice to men of other races. Then act on that list.

3. Have you learned to laugh a lot and be gracious in the face of mistakes? Can you begin believing that the desire to do the

right thing is in the other person's heart? How has God's *ḥesed* (kindness) been manifested in your life?

4. In regard to racial relations, what in your life is pleasing to God? What areas still need work? The author suggests you start slow and then get slower. For you, what is the first step?

Part of walking humbly with God is being in submission to His leading. After reading this book and answering the questions, it is time to ask God a question: "What would you have me do next?"

Notes

Introduction

1. Sam Keen, *Fire in the Belly* (New York: Bantam, 1991), 5–6.
2. George Barna, *The Frog in the Kettle* (Ventura, Calif.: Regal, 1990), 186–87.
3. Max Lucado, *No Wonder They Call Him the Savior* (Portland, Ore.: Multnomah, 1986), 36.

Chapter 1: All in the Family

1. Virginia Satir, *Peoplemaking* (Palo Alto, Calif.: Science and Behavior, 1972), 3–8.
2. Ibid., 4–5.
3. As quoted in Derald W. Sue and David Sue, *Counseling the Culturally Different* (New York: Wiley Interscience, 1990), 3.
4. Sue and Sue, *Counseling the Culturally Different*, 3.
5. Satir, *Peoplemaking*, 5–7.

Chapter 2: Warning: Being Black and Male Could Be Hazardous . . .

1. Quote taken from the MacNeil/Lehrer NewsHour, 18 January 1988.
2. "Rage of the Privileged," *Newsweek,* 15 November 1993, 57.
3. Ellis Cose, *The Rage of a Privileged Class* (San Francisco: HarperCollins, 1993), as excerpted in "Rage of the Privileged," *Newsweek,* 15 November 1993, 56.
4. Richard Lacayo, "Between Two Worlds," *Time,* 1989, 59.
5. William Pannell, *The Coming Race Wars?* (Grand Rapids: Zondervan, 1993), 47.
6. H. B. Clark and K. M. Clark, "Racial Preference & Identification," *Journal of Social Psychology,* 1939.
7. Derald W. Sue and David Sue, *Counseling the Culturally Different* (New York: Wiley Interscience, 1990), 99.

8. J. H. Turner and R. Singleton, Jr., "A Theory of Ethnic Oppression," *Social Forces* 56 (June 1978): 1001–8.

9. Ossie Davis, "English Language Is My Enemy," *Negro History Bulletin* (April 1967), 18.

10. Andrew Hacker, *Two Nations: Black and White, Separate, Hostile and Unequal* (New York: Ballantine, 1992), 181–82.

11. Ibid., 183.

12. George Gilder, *Sexual Suicide* (New York: Bantam, 1975), 129.

13. Noel Cazenave and George Leon, "Men's Work and Family Roles and Characteristics," M. Kimmel, ed., *Changing Men: New Directions in Research on Men and Masculinity* (Newbury Park, Calif: Sage, 1978), 244–62.

14. Ibid., 251.

15. Cose, "Rage of the Privileged," *Newsweek,* 15 November 1993, 58–63.

16. Ibid., 58.

17. Richard Majors "Cool Pose: The Proud Signature of Black Survival," *Changing Men* (April 1986), 17.

18. James Doyle, *The Male Experience* (Iowa: Wm. C. Brown, 1989), 286.

Chapter 3: Inside the Hearts of Men of Color

1. Lewis Smedes, *Shame and Grace* (New York: HarperCollins, 1993), 59.

2. Shelby Steele, *The Content of Our Character* (New York: Harper, 1990), 43–44.

3. Smedes, *Shame and Grace,* 107.

4. Ibid., 108–9.

Chapter 4: The Asian-American Man: The Model Minority?

1. Pan S. Kim, "Asian-Americans in Public Service," *Public Administration Review* 54 (May–June 1994): 285–90.

2. "America's Asians: The Glass Ceiling," *The Economist,* 3 June 1989, 23.

3. Howard Chua-Eoan, "Strangers in Paradise," *Time,* 19 April 1990, 33.

4. Quoted in *Asian Week,* 2 July 1993.

5. Joe Treen, "Death of a Visitor," *People,* 16 November 1992, 77.

6. Script quoted from Rita Chaundhry Sethi, *The State of Asian America* (Boston: South End, 1994), 239.

7. Quoted by Ray Chang in "Stereotype-Basher," *Transpacific* (March 1994).

8. Sethi, *The State of Asian America,* 243.

9. Tom Kagy, "Sex, Fists, Paranoia: The Confessions of an Asian American Man," *Transpacific* (January/February 1993), 44.

10. Ibid., 40.

11. Ibid., 42, 44.

12. Maria Root and Laura Brown, *Diversity and Complexity in Feminist Theory* (New York: Haworth, 1990), 191.

13 Kagy, "Sex, Fists, Paranoia," 40.

14. David Batstone, "Giving Up Innocence," *Sojourners* (November 1993), 20.

15. Catherine Meeks, "Rage and Reconcililation," in *America's Original Sin: A Study Guide on White Racism* (Washington, D.C.: Sojourners, 1992), 161.

Chapter 5: The American Indian: The Invisible Man

1. Vine Deloria, *Custer Died For Your Sins: An Indian Manifesto* (New York: Avon, 1969), 35.
2. Angie Debo, *A History of the Indians of the United States* (Norman, Okla.: Univ. of Oklahoma, 1970), 284–98.
3. Ibid., 2.
4. Ibid., 62.
5. Robert Bergmann, "The Human Cost of Removing Indian Children from Their Families," in *The Destruction of American Indian Families,* ed. S. Unger (Association of Indian Affairs, 1977), 38.
6. C. Attneave, "The Wasted Strengths of Indian Families," in ibid., 29–31.
7. Sally J. McBeth, *Ethnic Identity and the Boarding School Experience of West-Central Oklahoma American Indians* (Washington, D.C.: University Press of America, 1984), 73–81.
8. Steven Pratt, "Presentation on Indian Students and Reticence," Univ. of Oklahoma colloquium, 1984.
9. John Perkins, *With Justice for All* (Ventura, Calif.: Regal, 1982), 98.
10. Ibid., 98–101

Chapter 6: The Hispanic Male: The Mascot

1. Earl Shorris, *Latinos: A Biography of the People* (New York: Norton, 1992), xv.
2. Ibid.
3. Ibid., 15.
4. Manny Ortiz, *The Hispanic Challenge* (Downers Grove, Ill.: InterVarsity, 1993), 70.
5. Samuel Ramos, *El Perfile Del Hombre Y La Cultura en Mexico* (Buenos Aires: Espasa-Calpe Argentina, 1951), 55ff.
6. Eldin Villafane, *The Liberating Spirit* (Lanham, Md.: University Press of America, 1992), 1.
7. Ibid., 20–21.
8. Rudy Gonzales, *Prophets Denied Honor*, ed. Stephen Arroyo (New York: Orbis, 1980), 16.
9. Adapted from Villafane, *The Liberating Spirit*, 15.
10. Villafane, *The Liberating Spirit,* 13.
11. Justo Gonzales, *The Theological Education of Hispanics* (New York: Fund for Theological Education, 1988), 70.
12. Ortiz, *The Hispanic Challenge,* 83–84.

Chapter 8: Who Am I? Who Are You?

1. D. R. Atkinson, G. Morten, and D. W. Sue, eds., "A Minority Identity Development Model," in *Counseling American Minorities* (Dubuque, Iowa: W. C. Brown, 1989), 159.

2. Derald Wing Sue and David Sue, *Counseling the Culturally Different* (New York: Wiley Interscience, 1990), 100.

3. Ibid., 101.

4. Ibid., 106.

Chapter 9: A White Man's Identity

1. Derald Wing Sue and David Sue, *Counseling the Culturally Different* (New York: Wiley Interscience, 1990), 140.

2. Ibid., 114.

3. Ibid.

4. Raleigh Washington and Glenn Kehrein, *Breaking Down Walls* (Chicago: Moody, 1993), 200.

Chapter 10: More Than a Dream

1. Martin Luther King, Jr., "I Have a Dream," in *The Annals of America,* (Encyclopedia Brittanica, 1968), 18:157–58.

2. Derald Wing Sue and David Sue, *Counseling the Culturally Different* (New York: Wiley Interscience, 1990), 60.

3. Raleigh Washington and Glen Kehrein, *Breaking Down Walls* (Chicago: Moody, 1993), 204.

4. John Dawson, *Healing America's Wounds* (Ventura, Calif.: Regal, 1994), 151–52.

5. Ibid., 153.

6. Washington and Kehrein, *Breaking Down Walls,* 116.

For Further Reading

We Stand Together is one of more than a dozen books published by Moody Press that address the needs of men. Other books dealing with developing male relationships are the "Men of Integrity" booklets (each under forty-eight pages):

Accountability Among Men, by Bob Beltz,
Building Strong Male Relationships, by James Osterhaus
Masculinity at the Crossroads, by Gary J. Oliver
Why Christian Men Need Each Other, by Pete Richardson

Men looking at their identities as men, husbands, and fathers will enjoy three other booklets: *Eight Steps to Intimacy,* by John Trent; *Five Myths of Male Sexuality,* by Rick Ghent; and *Fourteen Keys to Effective Fathering,* by Ken Canfield. In addition, we recommend three major books in the "Men of Integrity" series, which are written specifically to men. The three titles focus on men knowing themselves and developing positive relationships with men and women:

Bonds of Iron: Forging Lasting Male Relationships, by James Osterhaus
Purity and Passion: Authentic Male Sexuality, by Rich Ghent and James Childerston
Real Men Have Feelings Too, by Gary J. Oliver

For men seeking to strengthen relationships with their wives and sons, we recommend these books:

Boys to Men, by Steve Lee and Chap Clark
Loving Your Marriage Enough to Protect It, by Jerry Jenkins
Tender Love, by Bill Hybels